THE SHAPING OF NEW ZEALAND

Above. "Distant view of the Bay of Islands", 1827-8 watercolour
by Augustus Earle. *National Library of Australia/Nan Kivell Collection.*

Front cover. "The Hutt Road taken at the Gorge looking towards
Wellington", engraving after S. C. Brees. (Detail only)
Alexander Turnbull Library.

Brougham Street, Wellington, 1889 watercolour by
C. Aubrey. (Detail only) *Alexander Turnbull Library*

Paul Hamlyn   AUCKLAND   SYDNEY   LONDON   NEW YORK   TORONTO

THE SHAPING OF NEW ZEALAND

by M.H. Holcroft

Published by
Paul Hamlyn Ltd
Levien Building
Cnr Airedale and St Pauls Streets
Auckland
New Zealand
© Copyright M. H. Holcroft 1974
ISBN 0 600 07277 0
Printed in Hong Kong

CONTENTS

The Land Emerging

The islands now known as New Zealand were once the coasts of a primeval continent. Geologists believe that the act of separation (an act which might have taken a million years) was completed early in the Cretaceous period, before the mammals which began to appear in that era were able to reach this part of the world.

It was the culmination, though by no means the end, of a long upheaval as chasms and troughs were formed on the floor of the Pacific. The disturbance continues today in subterranean tremors —severe enough, and sometimes calamitous, for men who feel the earth move beneath them, or hear a rumble of eruption, but insignificant as geological episodes.

New Zealand was isolated physically for at least 100 million years. A time-scale of this magnitude can scarcely be imagined. It was not "New Zealand" which emerged, but narrow strips of land, flawed and brittle, and intent upon a life of the rocks as slowly, very slowly, mountain ranges rose out of the sea.

In human thought, where all such processes must be compressed for study, mountain-building acquires grandeur; it is seen in imagination as a result of cataclysm, a world everywhere in commotion. But in fact the changes were gradual. They meant a slow displacement of atoms through erosion, a pressure growing beneath the crust of earth, and the restoration of balance through earthquake or volcano.

There is time, in a million years, for tremblings and shakings to become ordinary facts of nature, almost the conditions of stability.

Otira Gorge (van der Velden)
The primeval scene has not entirely disappeared. It was recovered here by an
artist who studied the rush and flow of a mountain stream, capturing on a
sombre day the movement of water that over thousands of years had made a
channel to the sea.

Only in human experience, where time has a remorseless velocity,
and the universe spreads immensely around our pin-point
consciousness, do these events take an appearance of calamity.

We have seen for ourselves, but without the detachment of a
cosmic observer, what happens if earth crumbles or moves at
unknown depths beneath the surface. Settlers in Wellington saw
it in 1855, when houses built hopefully of brick were strewn along
the ground, and a new platform of rock arose 1.5 metres out of the
sea. More recently, in the earthquake of 1931, 13 square kilometres
of land were lifted from ocean while smoke drifted over Napier
and the dead were sought in the rubble of collapsed buildings.

These events were disasters, to be recorded with awe in our
brief chronicles. It would have been no consolation for displaced
or bereaved persons to be told that they had witnessed and shared a
moment of change in a process which had been continuing for
hundreds of millions of years. Yet the response in Napier, when
afterwards the debris was buried beneath a new foreshore,
providing the foundation of an esplanade that became the city's
pride, was not unlike the response of earth itself when each new
subsidence alters and sometimes improves the total scene.

Landscapes then, were formed among hesitations and, fluidly. We
can almost see it happening still, as mountain ranges seem in the
shadows of afternoon to melt into valleys or slide towards the sea.

8

Te Tarata White Terraces (after G. Barraud)
At Lake Rotomahana a geyser played for ages down a hill, creating terraces like
a staircase, coloured white and pink, and delicately responsive to sun or moon.
A few artists painted them before they were obliterated by the eruption of
Mount Tarawera.

A million years ago, when the first creature resembling a man
stood upright and looked about him, perhaps at an African plain,
the landscape in New Zealand was not yet complete. It was nearing
completion (as we would see it) when primitive men began their
long migrations, travelling down from Asia to islands in the warm
seas, or taming their herds and flocks on the steppes where Asia
and Europe became a single continent.

The outlines at that stage would have been recognisable today.
Mountain ranges were there, and abrupt cones with fires still
smouldering, the craters open or barely sealed. Rivers from the
mountains, cutting deeper into rock, had carried shingle to build
up the coastal plains. Far in the north were drowned valleys.
Swamps and bogs had formed at the mouths of rivers which came
only a short distance, and steeply, from hills darkened by rain.

Mammals had been kept out by ocean, the great waters pouring
in as blocks of land fell away from the edges of an ancient
continent; but seeds floated across on currents of air, softly lodging
on plain and hillside. Over most of the country, as the rocks
became stable, a forest was established. It spread 1,200 metres
above the sea, and beyond the timber-line were shrubs and grasses
and small plants.

Many are there today, holding tenaciously to whatever soil
their roots can find. They are the indigenes among plants,

Mt Egmont, Taranaki (John Gully)
Taranaki's mountain, known today as Egmont, has an appearance of
completion: the almost perfect cone suggests that here at least the landscape
has reached an untouchable peak. But it is only 350 years since the cone erupted,
and energies that built the mountain are latent, not extinct.

11

including some which—like the extrovert family of daisies—have long been acclimatised in lowland gardens.

The forest was evergreen, and sombre. It was undisturbed by man or animal for a million years. Birds and insects were its only inhabitants. The cycle of growth and decay was shared by great trees, shrubs, ferns, vines and mosses, engaged in a silent but intense struggle for soil and sun. Some of the trees had longer lives than human empires. The stems of kauri rose high above the undergrowth, and stayed in cloud and sunlight for 2-3,000 years. Rimu survived for seven or eight centuries, totara and matai more briefly, but long enough to outlive European dynasties.

There can be few other parts of the world, if any, in which forest kept so long its pristine character. In Europe and Asia and the Americas, or the land masses from which those continents emerged, the mammals won supremacy in the evolutionary struggle, preparing the way for Man. Reptiles had ruled for 160 million years, reaching giant proportions. The more grotesque of these creatures left no traces here, though it is not impossible that fossil bones could some day be recovered from areas that were submerged when brontosaurs grazed at the edge of Godwanaland, the primeval continent.

There was, however, one reptile which reached New Zealand and miraculously stayed. The tuatara was small, a mere 60 millimetres in length. Its ancestors had been modest saurians, growing no larger than 1.8 metres, and are identified today as "beakheads". But smallness can be an aid to survival. The tuatara came before the dinosaur, and outlived him.

Naturalists believe that he may once have lurked on the mainland, and retreated to islands off the coast after the arrival of men, especially Europeans with their retinue of cats and dogs and weasels. But now he is as safe as an Act of Parliament can make him. He lives to a great age, drowsily, and with long hibernation. His metabolism is low, his third or pineal eye appears to be vestigial; but he can move quickly for a short distance when at night he hunts the unfortunate weta. As a "living fossil", found only in New Zealand, he has become an object of great scientific interest. For the general public he is an awesome link with the age of reptiles, a little dragon with an ancestry which goes back unimaginably to the mesozoic era, 200 million years mistily behind us.

In an environment free of predators, birds were safe on the ground, and many stayed wingless. One species, the moa, grew large enough to be fearsome, if men had been there to fear it. Yet it was a harmless creature, feeding hugely on grass and berries, and for thousands of years it lived and died peacefully.

Although the forest was undisturbed by grazing animals, it was not free from interference outside its boundaries. Large areas were destroyed by ash from volcanoes still active in the North Island, and by others now dormant. A different sort of rain, hot and searing, fell with deadly softness on trees rooted to the hillsides.

Like earthquakes, volcanoes provide outlets for pressures beneath the earth's crust, but for human witnesses they seem to require other explanations, and only mythology offers them satisfyingly when—in the face of danger—men revert to a primitive condition.

Forest in Papakura District (Dr C. Fischer)
On the outskirts of forest, where sunlight could break through, the trees and
ferns had exuberance of colour as well as of growth; but further in, as the
struggle for soil and sun was intensified, the landscape darkened beneath a
covering of green.

An earth tremor comes swiftly, sometimes with a drumroll
announcement, and is over in seconds; but a volcano is a spectacle,
a demonstration of power which restores men to their true place in
the hierarchies of Nature. Forces that work insidiously through
earthquakes are made visible in fire and steam and ash; and
although they may be less disastrous for human beings, they
illustrate graphically, and sometimes terribly, the slow building of
the land.

In some parts of New Zealand the volcanoes were extinct before
forest and grasslands were established. The twin craters of Banks
Peninsula, now known as Akaroa and Lyttelton, have been inactive
for 500,000 years, though it is a mere 15,000 since the sea invaded
them. Tussock and grass have long covered their hillsides, but they
keep in outline the lava-flow of primeval times.

Other volcanoes, especially in the north, are much younger.
Travellers in Northland cannot fail to notice rounded hilltops

across the landscape. A long chain, at least 26 in number, stretches from a district below Kaikohe to Matauri Bay. Some of them are ridged and terraced where Maoris built their fortifications. They are all volcanoes that were active as recently as 2,000 years ago, not long before the first Maoris reached New Zealand. Perhaps they were dwarfs, in comparison with Ruapehu and Taranaki; but huge boulders, strewn across the countryside, illustrate the power that used them.

Auckland also has points of eruption: its small hills, deceptively quiet above the suburbs, have thrown ash across the isthmus; and Rangitoto, youngest of them all, was active about 200 years ago. Taranaki or Egmont, most symmetrical of cones, has been quiet for only 350 years; and other craters—Ngaruhoe and White Island—are still open and smoking.

It is possible to see a little of what was happening when the land was steaming from hundreds of fiery vents. In 1886 Mount Tarawera, which had been dormant for 900 years, erupted without warning. Steam blasts reached Lake Rotomahana, destroying the Pink and White Terraces; and the surrounding countryside shuddered under a shower of ash, rocks and scoria. A hundred people died under the debris.

The aftermath produced one of the strangest sights now to be seen in New Zealand. In addition to craters which broke across the three domes of Tarawera, a series of small vents appeared in country around Rotorua. At Waimangu, particularly, may be seen two crater-lakes of unknown depth. They lie in a cloud of steam, with gas bubbling beneath the surface; and steam comes also, in jets and plumes, from cracks in the rock high above them.

This rock is heavily fissured; it seems to threaten at any moment to crack and subside, re-enacting in slow motion the larger subsidences of an ocean floor which helped to build these islands. A light earthquake (the Maoris nearby would call it "a small cough") could begin the movement. Similar movements have already taken place, though on a smaller scale. The outline of this remarkable landscape has changed so rapidly in recent times that new names have been given to features pointed out to tourists. "Gibraltar", for instance, became "Cathedral Rocks" only a few years ago.

From the crater-lakes a stream emerges and flows towards Rotomahana. It is like any other stream except for two things— the sound of water near boiling point, and the cloud of steam which attends its progress among scalded rocks. On the banks are small hot springs, spurting and bubbling with a chuckling sound, reminiscent of a passage for oboes in *The Rite of Spring*. Only human shapes are needed, contorted in the steam, to complete a spectacle which Dante could have used for his environs of Hell.

Historians describe human events, and in New Zealand they glance only briefly at the age of silence before the land was peopled. What indeed is to be said of emptiness? The primeval story is seen, properly enough, as a subject for geologists. History arrived with the first Europeans, fully formed in their books, memories and habits. Before them, admittedly, were the Maoris; but in academic minds (though less often today) they are outside history, or grouped with other Polynesians in marginal cultures that failed to become a civilisation.

Site of the Terraces, Tarawera (Charles Blomfield)
The Pink and White Terraces were created by energies which formed the landscape. In 1886 their fragile beauty was lost in a few hours beneath steam blasts from the craters of Tarawera. And the work of landscape-building was resumed.

Maoris think differently; and today, with increasing confidence, they are claiming their hold upon antiquity. The story of New Zealand, they say, began with a first landfall by Polynesian navigators. And although the occupation of a new country had features common enough in Western history, there were also significant differences.

Maoris were conscious from the beginning of the land as a living thing. Their mythology had come with them from Hawaiki; but it was strengthened here, and modified, by the interaction of natural and human events. Unlike Europeans of the 19th century, they had time to look at the land, to live with it, to bring its lakes and mountains closer to them through myths and legends, and even names, which made them both familiar and sacred. In a thousand years, or longer, they could enter a relationship with the country that was essentially religious.

Nothing of the sort was possible for land-hungry settlers, fresh from industrial Britain, and eager to build and be rich in a decade. Only later, when the effects of building could be seen, and the world as a whole had become overcrowded, did New Zealanders look backwards, with a sort of longing, to a primeval dreamtime.

Maori attitudes were crude as well as sensitive. We have learnt to idealise them, and therefore see them out of balance. Mammals had been excluded as potential bridges fell away into the deep Pacific; and when at last the way was open to them it was the animal with the big brain, master of all other species, who claimed the land. He came first as a Maori, and original sin came with him. The "noble savage" of the 18th century idealists had his full share of human frailty. But a stone-age culture allowed settlement to be gradual. We have learnt to be grateful that Maoris were here, undisturbed from outside, for at least a thousand years before Europeans came bustling down their gangways.

It was not the fault of settlers that ways of living had been learnt which placed them in conflict with Nature. Yet if history came slowly, it came now with a rush. Maori attitudes were seen to be primitive, and were expected to disappear. But they kept their power, as the tribes rallied, and as Maoritanga advanced in spirit where arms had failed; and slowly, yet ineluctably, they began to influence the thinking of Pakeha New Zealanders.

Maoris understood the need to co-operate with Nature, and peopled the forest with deities or spirits which had to be placated. Europeans, as will be shown later, co-operated only with season and soil, using them for their own purposes, and destroyed forest without fear or conscience. But this approach belonged to a time that now seems brief enough against panoramas of history, and briefer still if we go beyond history to the brink of that long and creative silence whence came the moulded islands we know today.

Foot Prints.

An abrupt transition is required from geological to chronological time. It could be compared nowadays with the re-entry into Earth's atmosphere of astronauts from outer space. Suddenly time presses; there is no more weightlessness, and minutes are significant.

The islands of New Zealand were formed in hundreds of millions of years; and after mountain-building, their landscapes needed millenia to reach the outlines we know today. They began to change again from the earliest days of human occupation, though for a thousand years, perhaps longer, the changes were gradual.

The tempo quickened after what was called the Migration of 1350, when the big canoes came down from Eastern Polynesia (whether by chance or design is still uncertain: the debate continues). It became faster still in 1769, as *Endeavour* sighted hilltops inland from Turanga on the eastern coast of the North Island. In the years between Captain Cook's circumnavigation and the beginning of organised settlement (a single lifetime), the European impact was stronger; but from 1840 onwards, in little more than 130 years, it became explosive. The landscape did not merely change under European invasion; it was transformed, until only in the Southern Alps, and in valleys beyond the end of roads, was something preserved from primordial times.

A few people were able to see the country in its pristine state. Archaeologists believe that groups of wanderers may have landed here a few hundred years after the birth of Christ. They would have been Polynesians, blown off-course on fishing expeditions, or adventurously seeking new horizons; and if they spent the rest of their lives here, they left no trace. Some may have returned to Hawaiki, taking with them a story of a land inhabited exclusively by birds.

This was happening about the time that emperors of Rome were driving German barbarians back into their forests, or building walls to keep them there. The civilisation of Greece was at an end, its influence still creative but dispersed; and the Roman Empire was passing the meridian of power. Out of the ferment of those times would come European history and its culminating wars.

New Zealand was unheard of in Rome, and without a name; and the men who first saw it, or landed on an empty beach, may have been too hungry or weary to see more than the food they needed or a place for sleep and shelter. They would also be frightened. The forest was dark and unknown to them; some of its birds called strangely in the dusk and through the night; and a wind across the treetops could have contained the voice of a god, a soft and whistling sound which only the *tohungas* of later times would hear clearly and understand. Everybody knew that the country would have its own spirits, jealous and watchful, possibly malignant. And how could strangers expect to placate them— unless perhaps the great Maui had already been this way? If we see more than that we are using our own eyes, our own knowledge, and not theirs.

The Polynesians were good seamen, unafraid of distance; and as a rumour spread of landfalls south-west of their own islands the groups became more numerous, and included women. Radiocarbon datings have confirmed human presence about 900 years ago, and the evidence of a sizable population at that time may indicate several centuries of settlement before the much publicised voyage of Kupe.

The early settlers are known today as moa-hunters, and their culture is described as Archaic, to distinguish it from the Classical period after the Great Migration. Their story is still being reconstructed from burial grounds and rubbish dumps which show that the inhabitants of New Zealand hunted the moa for food, used its bones for tools and ornaments, and reached a high level of stone age development.

They do not seem to have entered Maori tradition. In a chapter on New Zealand in *Vikings of the Sunrise*, Peter Buck refers only once, and very briefly, to the moa. "The Polynesian name of the fowl, *moa*," he writes, "was evidently applied to a large wingless bird which became extinct." There were small moas as well as large ones, and the people who speared and trapped them were hunters but not warriors. They had no need to be warlike in a country which offered ample living space and food.

Maoris of the Classic period were more aggressive. Buck suggests that they might have been reacting to a colder climate, a suggestion not implausible if it is examined against western history, wherein the most savage and implacable fighters have generally issued from inhospitable regions. The moa-hunters may not have forgotten how to fight; but seclusion and security had left them ill-prepared to withstand the people of the canoes—most of them,

Waikato (J. B. C. Hoyte)
Gradually, as the stumps of trees were cleared from hillsides, a certain balance
was reached between wilderness and farmland. Green fields in the Waikato
became greener still against hills rolling back to bush-covered summits.

perhaps, tested and toughened in inter-tribal conflicts which had
helped to send them out from Hawaiki.

Defeat, however, came slowly, in skirmishes rather than in wars,
and was almost certainly followed by assimilation. Maori tradition
may be quiet about the moa-hunters because Polynesians unsuccessful in war were submerged in the victorious tribes. "Nowhere in
the whole body of Maori tribal history," writes Andrew Sharp in
Ancient Voyagers in Polynesia (1963), "is there any genealogy of a
defeated previous family. All the surviving genealogies are of the
families which were still in power in historical times."

Some archaeologists believe that the moa-hunters had no
agriculture, but lived entirely by hunting and fishing. Hunters
are nomadic, following their game wherever it may be found; and
the fowl they wanted, large and small, were more plentiful in the
South Island, where the plains provided easy and ample grazing.
Nineteen species were found there; and it is in the south that the
largest camp sites and middens have been uncovered.

This suggests a picture of settlement very different from what
is known of Classical times, when the Maoris were always more
numerous in the north. It has been supposed that they were seeking
a climate closer to the one they had known in their ancestral
homeland. Yet if the moa-hunters, who also were Polynesians,
could flourish in the cooler south, so also could the tribes which
conquered them. The explanation, probably, was not a hunger

Tu Kaitote (G. F. Angas)
Maoris were close to the land and knew its sacred places. At Tu Kaitote, a pa
on the Waikato, the villagers lived under the shadow of Mount Taupiri. It
was a living presence, known to hunters, but with groves protected by *tapu*.

Wanganui Pa (J. A. Gilfillan)
Village life began to change for Maoris when Europeans arrived. In clothing,
especially, there were innovations and experiments, not always with happy
results. But the easy fellowship, the good humour and communal warmth, were
undisturbed—or were put aside only for the serious business of fighting.

for the sun, but the needs of the kumara, their staple food, which
could live only in warm soil and sheltered gardens.

It was this crowding to the north, no doubt, which caused
territorial disputes and ultimately the inter-tribal wars. There
have been reasons for war more trivial than the sweet potato. True,
the Maoris needed little encouragement to take to arms. Their
preference for hand-to-hand combat was significant. And their
code of behaviour, especially a need of retaliation expressed
through *utu*, a Mosaic concept of justice, had become an elaborate
framework for violence. But the violence was always there, as it is
and seems likely to remain, at the core of human nature.

The moa-hunters needed canoes to take them up tidal rivers
and along the coasts where forest was heavy; and therefore they
had to find tools. They became expert in making adzes, using
obsidian, basalts and cherts. Dr Roger Duff has divided the adzes
into six classes which indicate a wide variety of uses. But there is
no evidence that any of them were used for weapons.

In those days, then, the Polynesians moved freely up and down
their long islands; and already, as the rubbish dumps and oven-sites
grew around their resting places, the country began to show marks
of human occupancy. The moa-hunters knew Maui, hero and
demi-god, and therefore had the gift of fire, so that smoke began to
rise above clearings and coastal villages. In a dry season also there
might be flames, showing redly through the undergrowth and
licking at tall trees.

Maori Village, King Country (W. G. Baker)
The Maoris had trails through forest and across mountain passes; but their
journeys were made wherever possible by sea and river, so that trees were
undisturbed, or were used ceremonially for the making of canoes. Villages
inland were found by lake or river, always with canoes at the water's edge.

The earliest tracks were made. Harbours and lakes were
crossed in canoes, but had to be linked by trails which skirted the
forest and followed the summits of hills where trees grew thinly.
Maoris used the trails and extended them, long after moa-hunters
had disappeared; and in the South Island, when greenstone had
been discovered in rivers of the West Coast, a new track was made
through mountain passes.

Maoris also hunted the moa, perhaps using dogs they had
brought from Polynesia to run down the chicks and smaller birds.
But this was an additional source of food, eventually to disappear
as the moa became harder to find. From the beginning the Maoris
had forms of agriculture. They had brought with them the kumara,
the taro and the gourd; and of these the kumara, although needing
careful treatment in a colder climate, survived transplanting most
successfully and remained a favourite food.

Maoris of the Classical period snared birds and caught fish;
and to eke out their staple diet of kumara they crushed the roots
of fern. Their implements were primitive, but the *ko* turned over
the soil well enough, and a *kaheru* mounded it, in the hands of
villagers and slaves. All their agriculture was communal,
supported by ritual and invocation, and attended invisibly by
deities of the forest and the good earth.

The Maoris liked to move about, and even after European
settlement were inclined to seek new ground when the fertility
of a garden was exhausted. In earlier times, before tribal wars kept

them close to their pas, they had all the space they needed, and were free to wander. They were slow to lose this feeling that the whole land was theirs, and perhaps have not lost it today.

It has been estimated that 200,000 Maoris were living in New Zealand when Captain Cook arrived in 1769. Most of them were in the North Island; but the Fish of Maui could support them, and they treated the land carefully, avoiding sacred places, and sometimes using *tapu* as an unconscious form of conservation. Although they wandered freely, they travelled on foot or in canoes, so that journeys were slow, and wide areas—especially forest—were untouched by human footprints, or received them lightly.

There were no horses until Marsden landed two of them at Rangihoua on Christmas Eve in 1814, an event which onlookers found "the strangest thing in nature", especially when the reverend gentleman mounted one—a little stiffly, after all those days at sea in the *Active*?—and cantered down the beach.

Marsden's intentions were benevolent, and his work for the natives of New Zealand never ceased to be practical. He could not have known (or in the heat of that triumphant canter have had time or inclination to reflect) that he had closed forever an age of pedestrian travel, a thousand years in which men moved on their legs alone when the canoes were beached and they turned inland.

Thenceforward the trails would become wider and go further; and the way was open for the wheel, the true supporter of civilisation. Marsden could not have dreamed that the wheel would ultimately carry motor cars, the machines which more than anything else would bruise the landscape and destroy its solitudes. If he *had* known, he might not have been much disturbed, since he believed unshakably in "infinite wisdom", saying often that whatever God ordained would "in the end be best". In the meantime he had taken a large step towards the introduction of agriculture, in the European manner (he had landed cows as well as horses); and for the day, surely, that was sufficient.

The Maoris were ready for a wider range of farming. Marsden's protege at Rangihoua was Ruatara, a chief of the Ngapuhi tribe, and in his own right a remarkable New Zealander. He was one of those forward-looking Maoris who accepted the outside world, and indeed went out to meet it, working as a seaman on whalers and sealers, travelling to England in the hope of seeing King George III, and after the disappointment of his hopes going out to Sydney on a convict ship, an experience which might have been expected to weaken his good opinion of the British and their civilising mission. But Ruatara had a vision which could not be destroyed by hardship, indignity and brutality.

He stayed on Marsden's farm at Parramatta, learning about wheat and ploughs and horses; and when Marsden landed at Rangihoua to set up his mission in 1814 he was there also, full of plans for the conversion of his settlement into farms that would extend 64 kilometres from a town laid out in a European style. "His grand object," wrote Marsden in one of his journals, "was agriculture; he calculated that in two years he should be able to raise sufficient wheat for all his people and to supply other chiefs with seed, and in a short time to export some to Port Jackson in exchange for iron and such other articles as he might want."

Wanganui (Joseph Hamley)
Settlers unable to find land near Wellington were diverted to Wanganui, and a
small town was built at the river's mouth. Homes and warehouses stood baldly
where forest once reached the water's edge; but around the bend, and far into
the wilderness, the trees were still undisturbed.

This was in 1815, and Ruatara died soon after at the age of 28.
The Maoris did not send wheat to Australia; but 20 years later
they were exporting pork and potatoes (which in 1807 had already
superseded the kumara as their principal food).

If Ruatara had lived into old age he would have seen much of
his dream fulfilled. By 1857 William Swainson was able to report
that Maoris in the Bay of Plenty, Taupo and Rotorua (numbering
8,000) had more than 1,200 hectares in wheat, 1,200 hectares of
potatoes and nearly 400 hectares of kumara. They also owned
nearly 1,000 horses, 200 head of cattle and 5,000 pigs. Nor was this
the end of Maori enterprise: they were moving also into shipping,
eager to carry their crops to market as well as to grow them. By
1858 Maoris owned 53 small vessels registered at Auckland, and in
that year more than 1,700 of their trading canoes entered the
harbour.

Signs of progress vanished abruptly in the opening skirmishes
of the Maori-European Wars a few years later. Maori agriculture
was resumed long afterwards, and in a few places was barely
interrupted (the tribes of Taupo, for instance, had acquired 2,000
sheep and refused to leave them, believing that they would be
confiscated by the Government); but the sustaining vision, the
confidence with which Maoris were moving towards a place in the
civilised world, was gone, and could never be entirely recovered.

Ruatara's hopes were not for himself, but for his tribe, and in
a larger sense for all his people. He had seen what men could do

Waitohi Harbour (Sir Wm Fox)
In 1847, when William Fox painted this watercolour, the site of a new settlement
had been bought from Maoris at an inlet of Queen Charlotte Sound called
Waitohi. It was to be known later as Picton. Fox's painting caught a moment of
transition, the land almost empty as Maoris moved out and Europeans moved in.

with iron tools and machines, and he wanted New Zealand to have the use of them for its own advancement. It was, however, to remain essentially the country of the Maoris.

Europeans were welcome, if they behaved properly and traded fairly. They could live here, if they wished, and even buy some of the land in exchange for an appropriate number of axes (there had always been so much of it, anyway!). Maoris were ready to help them cut down trees and burn the undergrowth. They made raupo huts for newcomers, helped them to build houses, carried their goods across country, and worked on farms and in the homes of settlers.

Without them, settlement in later years would have been slower and more costly. But the Maoris did not see their own position as in any way subservient. They may have seemed uncouth and sometimes ludicrous to young ladies who wrote letters to Mama in England, describing with shudders—the words underlined —the appearance at their doors of savages dressed partly and oddly in European cloths, and looking like scarecrows.

In their own way, however, the Maoris were accepting civilisation, or what they believed it to be. Their leaders, including Ruatara, wanted a Maori nation made rich and strong by learning from Europeans. And in pre-settlement times there were Europeans who shared the vision. Samuel Marsden, writing in 1815, expressed his view that the islanders would "soon be ranked among civilised nations"; and he was thinking of the Maori people, especially those he had met and respected in the Bay of Islands.

In 1815, however, Ruatara already suspected that the Maoris would not be left to develop the country in their own way, or with limited aid from Europeans. Marsden mentioned this suspicion in a letter, and apparently believed it to be unfounded and even unworthy.

"These prejudices," he wrote, "originated at Port Jackson just before I sailed with him to New Zealand, from some person or persons, with the most dark and diabolical design, telling Duaterra [Ruatara] not to trust us, that our only object was to deprive the New Zealanders of their country and that as soon as we had gained any footing over there we should pour into New Zealand an armed force and take the country to ourselves . . . I frequently endeavoured to remove his fears, but to no purpose."

Marsden believed that the Maoris would be left to accept the benefits of Christianity, accompanied by the benefits of agriculture; and official thinking in London and Sydney would no doubt have supported him, since Britain was not in a colonising mood, and everything was happening a long way off, in parts of the world too remote to affect British interests, which as always were concerned with the balance of power in Europe.

There were to be changes of opinion; but in 1817, when plans for a colony in New Zealand were being discussed in Sydney, Marsden still saw it as acceptable only if it were "small" and comprised of "suitable persons . . . who would act in unity and conduct themselves with propriety".

On his second visit to the Bay of Islands, in 1819, his friend and protector Hongi Hika had armed his warriors with muskets and was rampaging through the north. Many chiefs at that time were

Port Nicholson & Petone (Charles Heaphy) (Detail only)
There was still much forest in and around Port Nicholson when Charles Heaphy
painted this scene in 1840, looking down towards the foreshore at Petone. It
was soon to be attacked, and cleared, by men landing from immigrant ships in
the harbour, or building huts at "Britannia".

Auckland from Mt Hobson (Hope)
Maori people, used to their enclosures, began to enter a strange new world as
Europeans built houses and roads on the outskirts of Auckland. Already, in the
1840s, these Maoris at Mt Hobson could have asked if ancestral lands were
being swallowed too quickly.

asking for an end of bloodshed, and saw European government as their only hope. Marsden was now inclined to agree; but it was the sins of Europeans which finally convinced him, in 1837, that action should be taken. He was shocked by what he saw at Kororareka. "Some civilised government," he wrote, "must take New Zealand under its protection or the most dreadful evils will be committed from runaway convicts, sailors and publicans."

If New Zealand had been rediscovered a hundred years before Captain Cook's first voyage, it might have remained a Maori country with an infusion of European blood. Cook himself, however, was preoccupied from the beginning with the prospects for European settlement; his reports to the Admiralty were obviously intended to facilitate plans for colonisation. He knew about conditions in England. The industrial revolution had begun, population was growing, and the masses were entertaining dreams of freedom and prosperity. It was a time of discovery and restless movement. The human race everywhere was responding—as the lower animals do—to strange scents carried as if by a wind across the plains and forests of the world.

As the scientific revolution began to move at a faster pace, and God received merely polite attention, the situation of a Polynesian people, emerging from a stone-age culture, and still believing in deities of earth and sky, was interesting but somewhat unreal. Their country was thinly populated, and apparently fertile; and in the interests of Progress, a word now acquiring sacred overtones, it should be brought into use for the advantage of mankind. And since the most enlightened part of mankind lived in Britain, and in a few favoured corners of the Continent, it was clearly from there that settlement should be planned and organised.

The confiscation of Maori land has been attacked, rationalised and defended, sometimes with passionate sincerity, sometimes cynically; but it must be seen now as a fact of history, a source of bitterness to this day, and producing influential ideas and attitudes as Maori and Pakeha live together, not always comfortably, in their multi-racial society.

By 1838, however, when Marsden died, Ruatara's dream must have been put aside long before, except by a few idealists. Two years later, as the New Zealand Company landed its first settlers, and Auckland began to grow in the north as if by its own volition, it was too late to dream of the future, unless in Pakeha terms. The landscape was now to receive a new sort of footprint—large and heavy, and with suggestions of permanence.

British settlers brought tools and methods shaped in thousands of years of shepherding and husbandry, and improved in the furnaces of Midland foundries. In the first 50 years, although dependent on horse-drawn vehicles and implements, and much manual labour, they produced results which still surprise their descendants. The South Island particularly, where large areas had been free of forest, and where the Maori population was too small to cause many delays in the alienation of land, echoed to D'Arcy Cresswell's "great shout of progress".

Nearly all the colonists wanted to be landowners; and the humbler immigrants, intended to work in their proper stations, moved as quickly as they could to small-holdings, and sometimes

Otira Gorge (after C. Barraud)
After explorers came road-makers and coaches. These were superseded by
railways; but one route, between Canterbury and Westland, was used long after
others had been closed. Until the Otira tunnel was opened, in 1923, a colonial
experience was renewed by timetable at the feet of the mountains.

to sheep-runs. When the last land had been taken on the plains,
enterprising men (the Aclands and Tripps) proved that high
country could carry sheep profitably. A later arrival in Canterbury,
John Grigg of Longbeach, did better by freeholding thousands of
acres of "impassable swamp" and converting it into "the best farm
in the world".

As new energy and money poured into the country, and a
colonial society grew robustly, the idea of a Maori enclave, nursed
by European mentors to an independent place among civilised
nations, was seen to be a dream of good intentions, a step or two
outside the real world of the 19th century.

The country was now showing effects of Pakeha invasion. Some
were bad, and threatened to be disastrous; others were beneficial,
introducing new and milder scenes of pasture, tree-guarded homesteads and marching hedges where once had been forest or uncouth
scrubland.

In all this development no aspect has received more attention
than the use of fire. It was drastic and dramatic, though reports of
it were sometimes exaggerated. Forest in the North Island was
often too thick and wet for firing. Settlers who wanted clear places
for homes and pasture had to make them by back-breaking work
with axe and saw. Once the clearings were made, smaller timber
and undergrowth could be cut down and dried for an autumn
bonfire.

Nelson 1841 (Charles Heaphy)
Maoris were at first excited, and then alarmed, by the speed with which
settlements were founded. This was the scene at Nelson in 1841, as depicted by
Charles Heaphy. Ships were arriving; cargoes were being landed; and house,
tents and wagons were awaiting the first wave of colonists, eager for action.

These activities were watched with interest by Maoris in the neighbourhood. They had seen fire on the edge of forest, or had heard tales of it from the elders; but it came usually from a burning pa, and was the end of a sharp encounter in which justice was done for wrongs committed against the tribe, perhaps a long time ago. The forest itself, Tane's domain, was sacred ground; and although trees must be taken for canoes, it was done in accordance with priestly injunction and in a ceremonial way which appeased the god.

Pakehas felt no need of reverence. They attacked the trees fiercely, as if they were enemies; and if they entered a primeval silence they went immediately to work, unafraid of what was there, or unseen, and hearing nothing strange in the sound of steel when that ancient silence was fractured.

The skeletons of trees soon lay blackened on hillsides. They may still be seen in places which came late into production; and nowadays also the remains of motor cars or trucks may be rusting at the bottom of the same paddock. Of the two sorts of skeletons, these are the more unsightly, offering no hope of renewal. The middens of this age will seem strange to those who in a distant future uncover glass and metal and plastic—just as durable, no doubt, as the bones and shells and adzes of the moa-hunters, and telling a larger story, but unlikely to win admiration as works of art from primitive hands.

The big burns were in the South Island, where thorn and tussock threw a tangled mat across large areas of plain and foothill. Settlers loved them, delighting like children in fires made lawful by the needs of soil, real or fancied. Lady Barker described one in her high-spirited way; and Samuel Butler, an observer more capable of detachment, said in *A First Year in Canterbury Settlement* (1863) that he had seen "no grander sight than the fire upon a country which has never before been burnt and on which there is a large quantity of Irishman [matagouri] . . . The flames roar, and the grass crackles, and every now and then a glorious lurid flare marks the ignition of an Irishman; his dry thorns blaze fiercely for a minute or so, and then the fire leaves him, charred and blackened for ever. A year or two hence, a stiff nor'wester will blow him over, and he will lie there and rot, and fatten the surrounding grass."

A much fuller description, deliberately orchestrated but powerful nevertheless, was given by H. Guthrie-Smith in *Tutira*, best of all books on the transformation of the countryside. Yet here, in the less fertile parts of Hawke's Bay, where Guthrie-Smith looked out from his lakeside homestead, the enemies were fern and manuka, locked together in a struggle for a shallow soil. Of these two, fern was perhaps more to be feared; it was the primeval growth and had awe-inspiring powers of recuperation.

Late in autumn, when the wind approved, it was set alight, and afterwards the land was sown with grass and clover. Almost immediately the fern, its roots still alive under the blackened earth, began to push green shoots above the surface. At this point sheep were moved in. They did not like fern; but there was nothing else to eat, and slowly—a little reluctantly—they nibbled across to the hilltop trails, crushing the fern and preparing the soil for a true pasture.

Southern Alps (after Heaphy)
Europeans were soon exploring remote places. Ships entered bays where only canoes were seen before; Maoris carried provisions for travellers and showed them ancient trails. Newcomers saw the mountains as alien shapes, giving them outlines that time would change or soften for their descendants.

Dr Greenwood's House, Motueka (S. Greenwood)
There was a half-way period in settlement when remnants of forest stood close
to homes and fields, their colours in contrast, and yet beginning to blend. The
large house in this picture, painted in 1852, was on a site which would now be
the centre of Motueka.

A burn could make virgin soil productive; but settlers came to expect too much of it, repeating the process annually, until even a native growth was discouraged. Young tussock no longer appeared, and barren patches began to spread below the summits of hills. Water streamed down to flooding rivers when the rains came; and erosion, a normal operation in Nature, accelerated until it became an ominous word in the vocabulary of farmers.

The use of sheep to remove scrub at Tutira may illustrate another aspect of the assault on landscape. Europeans did not come alone to New Zealand, or stay long without the retinue of animals which had become extensions of farming and family life. Maoris had done the same before them, and perhaps would have done more if mammals in Polynesia had been numerous. Only the dog came from Hawaiki, and the native rat, *kiore*, a smallish creature which fattened cleanly on berries, and was succulent when lifted from a steam oven.

The dogs were not strong enough as a breed to survive white settlement, especially the well-fed and aggressive animals loosed upon them; and the *kiore*, although said to be surviving in a few secluded places, has long been outnumbered and driven away by the grey and black rats whose ancestors came like shadows from Captain Cook's *Endeavour*, and were reinforced soon afterwards from the holds of whalers and sealers. Native dogs and rats passed lightly across the landscape, and left no footprints.

Europeans were much better attended. Captain Cook landed pigs, goats, cattle and a few fowl, wild and domestic. Although the cattle may not have survived, goats were elusive and venturesome, and moved rapidly inland. Pigs were also ready to settle, but were at once in danger. The Maoris found them good eating, and may have preferred an immediate feast to the slower rewards of breeding.

Cook expected them to survive. "I have at different times," he wrote on his last voyage in 1777, "left in this country not less than ten or a dozen hogs, besides those which Captain Furneaux put ashore, so that it will be a little extraordinary if there is not a breed, either in a wild or domestic state, or both."

Some writers believe that none escaped; others think they died in the north but lived and multiplied in the south. Whatever the truth may be, there is no argument about the name most probably used for wild pigs. In both islands they are "Captain Cookers". And whatever their source—ships trading for flax, or whalers— they were rooting among the fern (a food they relished) in large numbers when Marsden arrived in 1814. No matter where the missionary travelled, on all his visits, the chiefs brought him hogs as presents. And the food dressed and cooked when villagers entertained him was usually pork and potatoes.

Settlers also were grateful for wild pork, especially when mutton became monotonous; but it was characteristic of Englishmen that they should value the pig as a creature to be hunted. There was always a pretext: the Captain Cookers were too numerous, and were destroying pasture needed for sheep and cattle. At bottom, however, a love of the chase, for its own sake, was an abiding motive.

Pig Hunt, Wairarapa (S. C. Brees)
Pigs were landed by Captain Cook, and later by whalers. They were soon at home, eating fern with relish, but also showing a taste for potatoes. Settlers began to organise pig hunts, obtaining welcome supplies of pork, and at the same time enjoying ancestral excitements of the chase.

Edward Jerningham Wakefield revealed the colonial attitude in *Adventure in New Zealand*. He had become a storekeeper at Wanganui, and a large herd of swine was running nearby. "When I wanted to catch a number to send to Wellington, or to kill and salt down, a grand hunt took place." Wakefield had bred some dogs to the sport, using a mongrel breed "partaking largely of the bulldog, but mixed with the cross of mastiff and greyhound which forms the New South Wales kangaroo-dog".

It had become a fashion, he explained, for travelling settlers to have a pack of pig-dogs, "known for their strength, skill and courage, whether in fighting or hunting". Wakefield described the hunt with relish, and was precise on matters of form and procedure. For example: "A dog that persists in seizing the legs, or any other part, is generally shot by his owner, as the practice spoils the hams, and is considered contrary to rule." And finally: "The pig is rarely killed in the field, as it is considered more sportsmanlike to bring him in and show him off alive. . . ."

Wakefield's book was published in 1845, and the events he describes in it took place between 1839 and 1844 (he was regrettably casual with dates). He was of course a man of his times, though many people today would still be able to share his enjoyment of the chase, and approve his treatment of animals. The interesting fact, however, is that already, in the earliest years of settlement, there had grown up a code of behaviour, a ritual, for the hunting of pigs.

Eketahuna (C. Aubrey)
Skilled woodsmen from Scandinavia were brought as settlers to Eketahuna in 1872. The bones of trees had long been strewn across the landscape when this picture was painted 20 years later.

View of Native Settlement (A. J. Cooper)
Maoris were eager to use European implements and methods in agriculture.
The plantations of classic times were replaced gradually by tilled fields, with
fences to protect them instead of *tapu*. But agriculture kept its communal
character, as in this Hawke's Bay settlement, painted in the 1860s.

Sheep and cattle had been brought in from New South Wales,
and were being farmed in some parts of the country before the first
emigrant ships sailed from England. They were soon numerous,
and eventually became a multitude—the sheep, especially, to be
numbered in millions. These animals had to support the economy
for many years, in spite of markets that were at first remote and
always uncertain, and are still its principal prop and stay.

The land was cleared and gentled to make homes for them.
Within their enclosures, sometimes as large as a European
kingdom, they made their own trails, nibbled the pastures, and in
return supplied wool and carcases of a quality unsurpassed elsewhere in the world.

In all that wide and open country there seemed to be room for
flocks and herds to grow indefinitely; and in the 19th century, and
indeed until quite recently, nobody suggested that the body-wastes
of such a multitude could be anything but beneficial to the soil
which fed them. The cycle of growth, elimination and renewal
had a beautiful simplicity, especially for run-holders who fancied a
gentlemanly occupation while the sheep more or less looked after
themselves. It was too soon for scientists to ask if the countryside
might be under too much strain from a population of animals.

Nevertheless, the colonists liked to find practical or economic
reasons for the introduction of animals that could have no

Taieri Plains (Geo. O'Brien)
The landscape was not always treated roughly to make farms for settlers. On the Taieri Plains, as in some parts of Canterbury, swamps were drained to become rich pasture. The Otago settlement was barely 20 years old when these farmlands were painted in 1867.

immediate value for farmers. Thus the opossum was first liberated at Riverton with the intention of starting a trade in skins. The rabbit was freed as early as 1838, and was expected to provide food as well as sport. Nobody could have foreseen in those days a time when 40-hectare paddocks would be bare of grass, and riddled with burrows, the land itself seeming to move in the evening light as an immense army of furry creatures rose and scampered from intruding footsteps.

Weasels and their cousins, ferrets and stoats, arrived in the 1880s, ostensibly to control rabbits, though also to provide a certain amount of sport. It is alleged against these sharp little animals that they began to kill birds as well as their legitimate prey, and especially the weka. If this is true, however, they were surprisingly slow in finding and pursuing them. As late as the war years of 1914-18, wekas lived in large numbers 48 kilometres from Christchurch: their melancholy and haunting cry could be heard at dusk in gorges along the base of Mount Grey. It was perhaps their changing habitat, as human presence was felt more strongly, which drove these birds in depleted numbers to the wilderness.

Sport was the sole reason for liberating red deer at Nelson in 1851. And although it must soon have been evident that these animals destroyed native plants, prevented the regeneration of beech forest, and caused erosion of soil and river run-off, the

Canterbury Plains (Archibald Nicoll)
Sumner was planned as a subsidiary town for Christchurch, and for many years
cargoes were carried in small ships across its bar to Ferrymead. By the end of
the 19th century it had become a favourite resort, visited by crowds travelling
in double-decked "trailers" pulled by fussy little steam trams.

46

liberations continued (more than a hundred of them) until 1924. Seven other species were brought in during the same period; and thar and chamois, to the delight of hunters, were soon at home on the timber-line. It was still possible to believe in the 1920s that resources of land and vegetation were renewable and unlimited.

Colonists have been blamed for the introduction of animals now described as "noxious". They did not understand that creatures which provided sport in countries thickly settled and organised would range too freely, multiply alarmingly, and acquire new habits among alien trees. Criticism was based on hindsight, and not all of it remained valid as deer-farming—and poaching—became profitable in the 1970s. Historians may also remember 1973 as a year when the rabbit, most persecuted of creatures, became respectable again as influential voices were heard to say that rabbit-farming might be a useful source of food and profit.

It is not unusual for time to produce reversals of judgment, or even for the noxious to become edible. Colonists may have been hasty and unwise, acting without the knowledge that scientists can make available today, but they were not merely experimenting with acclimatisation: they were also trying to place around their settlements the texture of life as they remembered it from their first home in Britain. The British, and especially the English, had long depended on animals for sport and companionship. It was to be expected that settlers would need more than the flocks and herds which stocked their farms. The animal kingdom on which they depended, and which they loved to rule, helped them to believe that they possessed the land, removing its strangeness, and replacing it with a semblance of something ancestral.

Under all these pressures, then, the landscape changed quickly. There had been cleared places since the coming of the first Polynesians. Forest had always been close to them, or swamp and plain in their primal condition; but now the clearings became larger, and trees were under restraint, reserved for shelter, and growing in lines and belts instead of open profusion.

Sometimes there were no trees: the marks of tillage appeared, and roads and fences began to march across the plains. Order grew out of confusion; and gradually, as rough edges were made smooth, and stumps of trees were cleared from plundered hillsides, a sort of balance was established between wilderness and farmland.

Out of this balance grew an attraction of contrast. The green fields of Waikato became greener still against hills which rolled back into bush; and far in the south, on the plains of Taieri, pasture won from swampland was enhanced for the eye by the mountains which stood above it, their slopes moulded by primeval erosion into receptacles for a changing light.

Maori trails became roads, and new roads were taken through country which once seemed inaccessible. The mountains lost no grandeur, and may have gained some, when coaches began to carry passengers through a gorge in the Southern Alps. Always, for the Maoris and then for Europeans, there was so much land beyond the trails and the roads. Even when the settlements became towns, and the towns were called cities, and little red-roofed houses climbed the hills above seaside villages, the gifts of space were scarcely touched.

The Wharf, Collingwood (Unknown)
Life at Collingwood quickened when gold was discovered in the Aorere Valley.
Although there was no major rush, and results were disappointing, the township
began to prosper. In 1857, the peak year, 1,500 miners were in the district.
Events at Collingwood were a prelude to the invasions of Otago and Westland.

At Sumner, in Canterbury, the sea rolled across a bar to an estuary, as it always had done, carrying small ships to Ferrymead; and a pier was built in deep water alongside Cave Rock, a fragment of lava thrown long ago from the volcano that is now Lyttelton Harbour. Who was to know that the beach would change, under storm and erosion, until the pier stood on dry sand, and no more launches carried excursionists to an estuary grown too shallow for the entry of ships? These were changes, surely, for which man was in no way responsible? And the space was still there: you could look out from a promontory and take in all those plains, and beyond them the mountains, white and beautiful in a sky of ethereal blue.

It was the same in so many parts of New Zealand. The wilderness had been tamed, where necessary, and was unspoiled beyond the farmlands. A new and beautiful landscape had emerged from the balance between natural and man-made environment. Was not this a sort of evolution, offering a promise of security for the land and the people as the scars healed and the bruises were forgotten?

Perhaps it was; but it had taken place before the coming of the motor car, a third invasion in some ways more fateful, for the landscape, than the arrival of canoes and ships.

Entry of the Serpent.

In the beginning was the land alone, preserved so long from footprints and spoiling hands that men who saw it first would have to believe in an act of Creation. After wonder, however, comes acceptance; and once the scene is familiar, the human drama begins again to unfold, revealing a few central themes and their infinite variations. The serpent enters at last, innocent of evil, yet resuming its ancient symbolism.

Maoris had their legends, transmitted orally, and thus put together in the manner of the *Iliad* and perhaps the *Odyssey*. Orators of each generation added detail, or merely polish, until the tribes possessed a rounded story. There was time, in those centuries of Maori culture, for heroes to emerge and for large events to be recorded and embellished. With the arrival of Europeans, however, all was haste and commotion.

Events were reported instantly and judgments were made by individuals who stayed briefly and passed on, taking casual impressions or sharp little resentments to publishing houses in London. From the time of Cook's landfall, New Zealand began to suffer from too much documentation. It had been rediscovered while the Word was in the ascendant. Printing presses had to be fed; and a new and larger public, curious about distant regions, waited for books. A cloud of witnesses wanted to be heard, some in accusation and some in defence. There are few events in the 19th century on which judgment can now be unequivocal. Except in broadest outline, the country's history has become a continuing exercise in interpretation.

Anglican Mission, Rangihoua (unknown)
The first Anglican settlement was at Rangihoua. It was on poor land, and
better sites were available; but Marsden chose this one to give his people the
protection of a friendly chief, Ruatara, whose village was on a neighbouring
hillside.

No part of our history retains this need of examination more
strongly, or invites it more provocatively, than life in the church
settlements between 1814, when Samuel Marsden landed at
Rangihoua, and the arrival of emigrant ships in 1840. The story
has been told many times, and will be told again as every
generation sees it from new standpoints or relates it to changing
values. Its deepest interest is not religious, but moral and social,
as if it contained in seed or embryo much that was to emerge in
the New Zealand character in later times.

A hundred years ago a churchman might have assumed
automatically that missionaries were invariably good and wise
men, and that their opponents were worldly traducers. Judgments
for a long time were confined to two colours, black and white.
Even W. Pember Reeves in *The Long White Cloud*, written at the
end of the 19th century, was able to describe Marsden's achievement as "one of the pleasantest pages of New Zealand history".
"Pleasant" is about the last word for all that heart-breaking effort,
agony of spirit, and tribulation.

Reeves also saw the founders of the first mission station as
"sterling men". Keith Sinclair's, *A History of New Zealand*, 60
years later, stated bluntly that "the early missionaries bickered

incessantly and bitterly among themselves. Within twenty years three had to be dismissed, one for adultery, one for drunkenness, and one 'for a crime worse than either'."

By then, however, Dr Hocken had acquired Marsden's manuscripts from the Church Missionary Society, and after years of editing and preparation (by Professor John Rawson Elder) the collection had been published. Facts that were once hidden or decently veiled were in the open, and events and lives which had seemed to have a story-book serenity were brought closer to the truth of human experience.

Today, then, church settlement may be seen in perspective, and the wider scene makes it more significant. It is mainly a story of the Church of England missions, with some assistance from Wesleyans. The Catholic Church was not founded here until Bishop Pompallier arrived at Hokianga in 1838, and by that time the missions were finding their place in a wider community, and the ordeal by fire was ending.

The setting throughout was in the northern part of the North Island. Notable figures emerged afterwards and elsewhere, especially Octavius Hadfield and Bishop Selwyn; but these men were outside the drama which grew around Marsden. True, both of them worked at Waimate in its later years: the settlement was for a time Selwyn's headquarters, and Hadfield was ordained there in 1839. But the gentle and much-loved Hadfield was to find his life's work in the Manawatu and at Wellington, among events far removed from foundation troubles in the Bay of Islands; and Selwyn would need both islands, and a brand new diocese, to contain him.

If the Mission to New Zealand were seen as a play or a novel it would lean upon a strong cast of characters. The central figure was Samuel Marsden. Never far behind him was Hongi Hika, most powerful of all chiefs among the Ngapuhi, and a figure as Biblical as Marsden. He was a man of violence, gathering into his own impressive person the Maori passion for war, delighting in battle for its own sake, and in his coat of mail—the single present he had saved from King George's beneficence—controlling his campaigns with a tactical skill which in another time and in another country might have placed him among the great captains of history.

He was also, like Job, a man without hope. His last and fatal campaign was undertaken when misfortune began slowly to crush him. The more he succeeded abroad, the more certainly he suffered at home. His eldest and favourite son died in battle, a sacrifice to ambition and vengeance; his eldest daughter sickened and died of tuberculosis, a white plague that came with the Europeans. Her husband, impatient with a sick woman, was taken in adultery with Hongi's favourite wife, who promptly hanged herself. A second wife was killed, in accordance with tribal custom (though against Hongi's wishes) to atone for the death of the adulteress. And some of his own people, sensing his decline and fall, began to practise *muru*, taking what they could of his property in the belief that a man who had lost so much could only appease the gods by losing everything.

Meeting with Hongi (Augustus Earle)
Hongi landed at Kororareka after his last battle. At the head of the beach he
sat apart from his followers, attended only by wife and daughter (for his wounds
made him *tapu*). Augustus Earle, who later painted this scene, spoke to him
through an interpreter, conducting a bold and dramatic interview.

These afflictions impelled Hongi to seek relief in a new home. The place he wanted was at Whangaroa, already occupied by Ngatipou; and it was while he was driving these people from their strongholds that Hongi received the wound from which soon afterwards he died. Before this, however, he made a last appearance at Kororareka, crossing the bay in several large canoes, and spreading alarm among local tribesmen. His arrival was also witnessed by Augustus Earle, the wandering artist and author of *Narrative of a Nine Months' Residence in New Zealand* (1832), who immediately found an interpreter and hastened a mile from the village to "pay our respects to this celebrated conqueror".

One result of an unusual interview was a picture, perhaps the best known of all Earle's paintings, and now at the Alexander Turnbull Library in Wellington. It also produced a question which has a familiar sound today, though in 1828 it had more pertinence: "Finding we were newcomers, he asked us a variety of questions; and, among others, our opinion of his country."

Marsden and Hongi were principals, and larger than ordinary men; but in the background, and sometimes moving to the centre of the stage, was a mixed crowd of missionaries and artisans, chiefs and tribesmen, traders and whalers. Some of them—Henry Williams and Thomas Kendall among the missionaries, and certain chiefs—grew in stature, for good or ill; others faded quickly into anonymity and silence. Yet again and again they bring into a quiet room a murmur of life in village and settlement, confused sometimes, and then sharpening into the clarity of an event or insight which in its moment produced a lasting power. And always in the background is a sound of sea and forest, sometimes indistinguishable when a wind drives across the bar at Hokianga to the kauri groves beyond, or sweeps along empty beaches at the Bay of Islands.

The source of this power is the writings of Samuel Marsden, his journals and letters, collected in what is surely the best of all books on early New Zealand. *The Letters and Journals of Samuel Marsden*, edited by John Rawson Elder (1932). But the book cannot be separated from the man who wrote it, sometimes piecemeal, in notes scribbled on scraps of paper while he rested in firelight at a village in the interior of the island, with spears in the ground about him and sleeping natives nearby.

Only a superficial reader could know or judge him instantly, or fail to respond to him as an exceptional human being. It is possible to dislike and yet to admire him. In his lifetime he was loved and hated, as all men are who attempt large exploits. Long after his death he continues to suffer from detraction and uncritical praise. But nobody can ignore him, or safely decry his work for New Zealand.

Critics sometimes detach him from his own times, ignore his personal background, and judge his actions by our present standards. Much has been made, for example, of his severity as a magistrate in Sydney. And indeed he was severe: he once ordered a young Irishman to receive 300 lashes. The man had refused to disclose a hiding place for pikes that political prisoners hoped to use in an insurrection; but the punishment was hard, even for those

Falls near Kerikeri (Lejeune & Chazell) (Detail only)
In 1824 the falls near Kerikeri were painted by Frenchmen, more concerned with
detail than with power. But the picture has historical interest, and a certain
charm, while Frenchmen dressed for the streets of Paris stay immovably by a
New Zealand river.

Kororareka (S. C. Brees)
Not far from the mission settlement at Rangihoua a few Europeans, mostly disreputable, were living at Kororareka. Whalers and traders anchored offshore, bringing problems for the missionaries as they tried—for a long time in vain—to convert their Maori neighbours.

times. Leniency was not unknown in the later years of the 18th century. Captain Cook, who needed firm discipline for the safety of a ship at sea, seldom ordered more than a dozen lashes. Why should a clergyman, preaching a gospel of love and forgiveness, become inflexible when he left his pulpit to take a place at the bench?

Obviously it is unprofitable to discuss Marsden without looking first at a few biographical facts. Like Cook, he was a Yorkshireman, the son of a blacksmith and crofter. He was 20, and had known nothing but hard work at the forge and on the farm when a scholarship allowed him to complete his education at a grammar school and Cambridge. Marsden was then appointed chaplain to New South Wales, a post that few clergymen would have wanted. He was ordained and married, and at the age of 28 went off with his bride to take up his first ministry—in a convict settlement.

It was the young farmer, a man of strong physique and character, more than the inexperienced clergyman, who survived that harsh probation. He was a man of unshakable faith. There may have been something physical, an extension of his innate stubbornness, in his hold upon the gospel. Faith was part of himself, and therefore not to be surrendered. He was transparently an Old Testament man, accepting a Mosaic discipline; and throughout his life he had a personal relationship with God, as if he felt himself to be a prophet in the presence of Jehovah.

God's will must always be accepted; but sometimes, as authority settled upon him, he came close to questioning his Master's judgment. In 1823, when Marsden was compelled by the wreck of the *Brampton* to stay longer in New Zealand than he wished, he nearly wagged an admonishing finger towards the Heavens. "I am very anxious now," he wrote, "to return to my family and congregation, but have no prospect. I may be detained for months. This is a very dark dispensation. I know the Lord is too wise to err and too kind to afflict willingly. At the same time I feel an inclination to murmur and complain . . . The loss of the *Brampton* appears to me very mysterious. No ship was ever lost in the Bay of Islands before—the harbours are so commodious and fine . . . I know nothing happens by chance, and, therefore, it was the Divine will that she should be wrecked for reasons which man cannot explain. Therefore, Thy will be done!" It is difficult not to feel that the meekness was perfunctory.

Marsden never ceased to be a farmer, a fact which helps to explain the character of the mission settlements. In 1802, eight years after his arrival at Port Jackson, he had 263 hectares near Parramatta. A visitor was amazed that "such a short time should have sufficed to cut a flourishing farm out of the primeval eucalyptus forest and wild bush". There was probably less amazement when it was learned that 10 convicts had been assigned to work on the property. Nevertheless, Marsden knew what had to be done; it was for no frivolous reason that he came to be known as the most practical farmer in New South Wales.

The farm at Parramatta has a special place in New Zealand history. It was there that Marsden received the sons of Maori chiefs. From their earliest acquaintance with ships they had become

Entrance to Bay of Islands (Augustus Earle)
Samuel Marsden sailed past these headlands into the Bay of Islands in
December 1814. Also on board his brig, *Active*, were three missionaries and
their families, two sawyers and a smith, some cattle and sheep, two mares and
one "entire" horse. The organised settlement of New Zealand was beginning.

bold and eager travellers, working their passage on whalers and
smaller vessels trading for flax. Marsden took some of them into
his home, admired their physique and quick intelligence, and
began almost at once to plan the conversion of their countrymen.

Ruatara stayed at Parramatta for nine months in 1810,
recovering from hardships on his unsuccessful visit to England,
and learning to grow wheat. Here also came Hongi, Ruatara's
uncle, listening politely to Christian discourse, but thinking mainly
of war.

Marsden's interest in farming was carried over into his dream
of a New Zealand mission. He had learnt the Scriptures, and could
quote them fluently and with conviction; but he was no theologian.
"I am fully employed on one duty or another," he wrote from
Parramatta, "so as to have few idle moments. I have hardly time
enough for the study of divinity. There are no religious
disputations in the Colony. We are not called upon to defend any
particular points of doctrine, but to declare the plain and simple
gospel. This is easy to be done where the power of godliness is felt
upon the soul." And that was how it would be in New Zealand.

Waimate Mission House (Thos. Gardiner)
At Te Waimate, 24 kilometres from the Bay, work began in 1831 on three mission houses. One became Bishop Selwyn's palace in 1842. It was altered in the 1870s, but the hipped roof and dormer windows have been restored. The "Old Vicarage" is the only surviving house of the first inland mission.

Marsden's plans were accepted in London by the Church Missionary Society, but it was not easy to find suitable recruits. New Zealand was seen then as a place of darkness and savagery; no clergyman wanted to go to a country "where they could anticipate nothing less than to be killed and eaten by the natives".

Eventually two men came forward: William Hall, a shipbuilder, and John King, a ropemaker. Marsden had no hesitation in accepting them. He had always believed that religious teaching among the heathen should be based on civilising crafts, and especially agriculture. The ideal missionary, in his view, had a Bible in his pocket and both hands on a plough.

The attack on the *Boyd* at Whangaroa, and the massacre of her crew by tribesmen revenging an injury, delayed the start of the mission. In 1814, however, Marsden was at last able to sail for the Bay of Islands in his brig, the *Active*; and Hall and King—less ardent, perhaps, after prosperous years in New South Wales—went with him, accompanied by wives and children. Also on the ship was Thomas Kendall, a schoolmaster who had given up a good living in England to teach the gospel in New Zealand.

In the Bay of Islands, on December 20, Marsden invited local chiefs to come aboard the *Active* for breakfast. Afterwards, they were given presents—an indispensable gesture—and the missionaries were introduced. At the same time, wrote Marsden, the chiefs "were informed what duty each of these persons were appointed to do—Mr Kendall to instruct their children, Mr Hall to build houses, boats, etc., Mr King to make fishing lines, and Mr Hansen to command the *Active*, which would be employed in bringing axes and such other articles as were wanted from Port Jackson to enable them to cultivate their land and improve their country." Not one of these men was a clergyman, though Kendall was a lay catechist, and was to be ordained seven years later in England.

The practical character of the mission, thus established, was never lost, even when its spiritual activity was strengthened years later by the recruitment of an ordained clergyman. The Rev John Butler came in 1819, and was its superintendent until 1823, when Marsden suspended him for alleged drunkenness. Not until the arrival of Henry Williams, in 1823, did the missionaries have a strong leader, a little like Marsden himself; and by then, after nine years, the settlements were unchangeably in the mould that Marsden had fashioned for them.

His philosophy was simple and straightforward. The "temporal situation" of the New Zealanders, he wrote, "must be improved by agriculture and the simple arts in order to lay a permanent foundation for the introduction of Christianity. It may be reasonably expected that their moral and religious advancement will keep pace with the increase of their temporal comforts." The connection between comfort and morality was apparently based on intuition rather than experience.

Marsden made seven visits to New Zealand, exhorted and chided the brethren, bought land from the chiefs—for an appropriate number of axes—on which to build settlements at Kerikeri, Paihia and Waimate, and became the first European to

CMS Station, Kerikeri (Lejeune & Chazell)
The mission station at Kerikeri was five years old when it was visited in 1824 by a French corvette, *La Coquille*. Artists on the ship who painted this scene gave it a stylised treatment, reproducing the contours without seeing beyond them.

explore the interior. His travels were extensive and strenuous, even for a generation of prodigious walkers. He moved without fear and without harm among the tribes, discovered Manukau and Waitemata, and gained a vast knowledge of the Maori people, their laws and customs. In spite of cannibalism, and signs everywhere that the "Prince of Darkness" was abroad in the land, he admired and loved them, seeing them as children perhaps, but mainly in the sense that all men are children in the eyes of God, his Master.

These visits, although often lasting several months, were interludes in the larger story. For most of the time Marsden was more than 1,900 kilometres away, doing his best to keep in touch with the mission, but physically remote. If the missionaries had all been Marsdens, there would have been no serious difficulties. In general, however, they were ordinary men who had to live in isolation from their own kind. They were disliked by Europeans, transients and a few settlers, at the Bay of Islands; and their relationship with the Maoris was ambiguous.

"In thirteen years," Marsden once wrote with satisfaction, "no man, woman or child who was sent out to work [at the mission] has died or had a bone broken, though living in the midst of cannibals." It was indeed a notable fact, though it said more for the Maoris than for the missionaries. And its significance would

Otaki (Wm A. McCleverty)
Octavius Hadfield was ordained at Waimate, but soon afterwards took up his mission at Otaki. In this picture, painted in 1852, may be seen the church known at Rangiatea, begun in 1844 and finished five years later. The mission had then become influential among the Otaki tribes.

have been plainer if Marsden had mentioned a further truth—that in the same period no natives had been converted to Christianity.

The missionaries could not reach the imagination of people with a rich mythology and—in their own language—a command of words beyond anything to be expected from half-educated artisans. Tribesmen would have nothing to do with Hell, which in those days still oppressed the Christian mind. They believed that men suffered enough in this world and that happiness hereafter should be universal. The idea of one god instead of many was unacceptable. "We are of a different colour to you," they said to Marsden in a debate he reported faithfully to the Church Missionary Society, "and if one God had made us both he would not have made such a mistake as to make us of different colour."

The creation of the world, as told in the book of Genesis, could not weaken their preference for Maui, the fisher of islands. They listened attentively, as always, and were disconcertingly shrewd in argument. But their attitude to the missions was essentially practical. They agreed wholeheartedly with Marsden's faith in agriculture and the "civilising arts", and they wanted him to have every opportunity to establish them in New Zealand. The settlements might not be seen as centres of spiritual power, offering a revelation; but they could provide goods—blankets, axes, spades

Kororareka Beach (Mrs Wood) (Detail only)
Kororareka looked good from the water, especially to ocean-weary eyes, and
early travellers found the beach idyllic. But the settlement was small and
rough, with a liberal sprinkling of grog shops, and some runaway sailors and
convicts.

and (for a time) even firearms—that the natives cherished. They were seen as links with a world from which came a flow of interesting and useful articles; and although the supply was sometimes disappointingly thin, it could always be renewed.

Unlike the whalers and beachcombers, the missionaries asked little in return—some land perhaps, and labour, but often nothing more than goodwill, a commodity the Maoris were able to provide in abundance. In the bad times also, when Hongi was leading war parties north and south, the settlements could offer asylum to runaway slaves. And finally, missionaries had the most important of all the Pakeha gifts, an understanding of the written or printed word. Maoris wanted literacy more than religion, and in the later years of the missions they sought it in growing numbers.

In these circumstances it was not surprising that missionaries sometimes felt confused or inadequate, and fell into sinful habits. Thomas Kendall, most interesting of the early arrivals, came to believe that there could be no progress until missionaries understood the Maori language and were able to prepare translations of the gospel. He learnt the language himself, studied Maori custom, and passed gradually from study to imitation, competing for the favours of a village girl, and taking her as his mistress.

The girl's family was gratified, accepting a useful connection and dreaming of unlimited supplies of *taonga*. Kendall's colleagues drew away from him, outraged and disapproving, and wrote letters to Parramatta. Marsden judged the sinner promptly and severely, offering no hope of forgiveness. "His mind has been greatly polluted," he wrote, "by studying the abominations of the heathens. . . ."

Marsden was called upon increasingly to admonish and punish his weaker brethren. In spite of warnings, they persisted in trading privately, taking hogs, potatoes and Indian corn as barter to the captains of ships. Marsden chided them until they promised to end the practice. "We never find a man engaged to build a temple selling pans," he wrote in 1819.

Five years later, still admonishing, he had to impose strict regulations. If trade was necessary, the missionaries must buy and sell as a body, not as individuals. All dealings with the masters of ships must be undertaken by two members of the settlement's committee, who could be expected to strengthen each other against offers of strong drink and other temptations; and every transaction had to be recorded in a book kept specially for the purpose. The missionaries were unhappy, and had good reason to murmur. It was no fault of theirs that the "settlement system", imposed on them by Marsden, had failed. If they could not be self-supporting, how could they survive, and keep faith with the natives, without a little trade on the side?

Marsden was adamant, especially over a trade in muskets, which he never ceased to condemn. Kendall opposed him, pointing out that hatchets, which were given to the Maoris in large numbers, were used as weapons. He said also that the tribes could buy guns freely from whalers, and that the missionaries were placed at a serious disadvantage. Marsden dismissed all such arguments as specious and unworthy. Although he might have been unreasonable

Mission House, Moturoa (unknown)
Although the mission settlements were founded in the Bay of Islands, their later
history included pioneering work, and sometimes tragedy, in other areas. This
mission house at Moturoa, in Taranaki, was the home of John Whiteley, a
Wesleyan missionary killed by a war party in 1869.

about trade generally, he showed moral consistency on the sale of guns. A traffic in arms has always disturbed the Christian conscience; and in New Zealand, when the tribes were eager to take up old quarrels with new and better weapons, it became infamous in the hands of pious men.

These were difficult times for Marsden, an aging man who began to feel the effects of unsparing effort and much hardship. He appeared to be inflexible, and no doubt he liked to have his way in all things, inside and outside his church. Beneath the habit of authority, however, he may at last have needed support and reassurance. It had always been easier to judge than to explain; but now, instead of obedience and contrition, he had to face opposition and argument. A querulous note crept into his journal after a confrontation with Kendall: "It is very distressing to have to do with unreasonable professors of religion. I have always found it more easy to deal with unreasonable and wicked men. . . ."

The settlement system was strengthened when a mission was founded at Waimate, an excellent farming district, and 24 kilometres from temptations of "the shipping". Further progress was made by Henry Williams, who supplied badly needed leadership. In 1826 he built and launched at Paihia the *Herald*, a vessel big enough to trade along the coast; and although it was wrecked two years later, he had shown that the settlements could function independently.

These were practical achievements. Were they large enough, after 12 years, to justify all the efforts and sufferings of well-intentioned but sometimes ineffectual missionaries? Was not the main purpose of the mission, a spiritual one, still unfulfilled?

There was no time for the missionaries to succeed in relative isolation. It was ironical, perhaps, that success came at last with the colonists. Christianity was brought in ready-made, as part of a European community which Maoris wanted (or needed) to join, and not through missionary zeal. Yet the long ordeal at the Bay of Islands may not have been wasted. The work of the missions was slow, and sometimes misdirected; but it was shown at last, in the climax of the musket war, to have become influential.

The church settlement at Rangihoua was four years old when Hongi returned to Port Jackson with presents from King George IV, whom he had seen in London. He stayed with Marsden at Parramatta; and there is a story, perhaps apocryphal, that he quarrelled at table with another chief on a question of *utu*, and told him darkly to go home and await retribution. Soon afterwards he sold his presents for muskets and ammunition, and was allowed to take them to New Zealand. He was Marsden's friend and protector; but friendship had not brought conversion. The warrior lived only for war, and one pretext was as good as another: the ramifications of *utu* were inexhaustible.

From the beginning, the church settlements had depended on the goodwill of Hongi and his allies; and in the next 10 years, when thousands of tribesmen died in battle and massacre, and ovens were often smoking gruesomely, the missionaries survived with nothing worse than a few alarms and much anxiety.

70

Wahapu (J. Williams)
A ship's carpenter, Gilbert Mair, helped Henry Williams to build his mission
vessel, the *Herald*, at Paihia. Afterwards he set himself up at Wahapu, opening
a store and repairing ships. His house on the hillside expressed authority and a
growing prosperity.

The biggest danger had to be faced by the Wesleyans. They
had set up their first mission at "Wesleydale", near Whangaroa,
in 1823; and in 1827, when the Ngapuhi were moving against
Whangaroa for Hongi's last battle, they received a visit from
marauders. The missionaries lost their property in scenes of
plunder and confusion, and were in danger of their lives. Their
two leaders, Nathaniel Turner and John Hobbs (who behaved
courageously throughout) set off with 14 other persons, including
native helpers, on a long walk to the Anglican settlement at
Kerikeri.

On the way, tired and stumbling, they rounded a corner in the
track to see a war party moving towards them. Several hundred
men "were coming down in one dense mass with the utmost silence
and order, armed with muskets, bayonets and long-handled
hatchets". The missionaries expected to be killed, but were
protected by a friendly chief, Patuone, in a remarkable show of
authority.

"The instant he saw us turn the point, he turned round upon
the people and commanded them to stop; and never before in
New Zealand did I see so much authority exhibited, and . . . so
promptly obeyed. Some few pushed forward a little, but he instantly
pressed against them with his spear; . . . Some others ran into the

water to get past him, but he was in the water with them in a moment, and having stopped the people he told us to come forward towards him, which we did, and he then told us to sit down. Patuone and several other chiefs then came and rubbed noses with us as tokens of their respect, friendship, or goodwill."

This was in 1827, and by that time the "protective" system, through which missionaries relied on the goodwill of powerful chiefs, was under strain. The chiefs were still friendly, still hoping to benefit from the missions; but they were entangled in alliances and feuds, preoccupied with their campaigns, and increasingly anxious about their losses.

It may seem remarkable, in retrospect, that the mission settlements were allowed to remain almost untouched at the heart of so much violence. As the alliances changed or crumbled, the missions themselves might have been expected to collapse in dust and ruin. But they survived; and in the end it was the missionaries, and especially the intrepid Henry Williams and Richard Davis, who took the initiative in peace talks at Waima in 1828. By then, admittedly, Hongi was dead, and the tribes—all armed with muskets, and weary of bloodshed—were unable to see hope or profit in stalemate. But the missions justified themselves forever on that single occasion.

The achievement was not followed, as the missionaries hoped, by widespread conversion. Maoris came forward to be baptised, and the Church gained ground; but final success was to come as part of the colonising process. Church settlements in the Bay of Islands may be seen as bridgeheads, though this was a function the missionaries (who feared the approach of colonisation) would not have chosen or relished.

In a sense, perhaps, they were setting up outposts of respectability. The best of them were sincere and devout men, but others were of limited intellect and imagination. They had qualities of their time, country and class: mediocrity, a practical turn of mind, a distrust of unorthodoxy in creed or behaviour, a courage not unrelated to obstinacy. The story of the next century, and beyond it, was to show that these qualities had found in New Zealand a congenial soil.

Intruders & Forerunners.

Travelling men have always felt the attraction of islands. The captains of ships, hunting whales or seeking cargoes, turned to them for haven or trade. Fugitives saw them as places beyond the reach of gaolers, where a man might learn to live again. Unknown wanderers, drifting from one port to another, expected from them a fortunate landfall, or a dream of women, soft-voiced and welcoming.

Until recent times, also, they promised insulation from moral or economic epidemics. Insulation could mean security. It might even, for inquiring minds, be a setting for a new start in philosophy, a search for Erewhon which might ultimately change the world. For men who go to islands take the world with them, and having attained insulation turn outwards again, and will not rest until they have impressed or influenced some part of the human swarm they professed to despise.

In an interval of 70 years, between 1769 and 1840, all such people could seek what they wanted (and sometimes find it) in the islands of New Zealand. Whalers reached them soon after Captain Cook, and were anchoring in northern harbours before the end of the 18th century. There were also navigators, hoping to extend Cook's achievement. In 1791 George Vancouver was at Dusky Sound in the *Discovery*, very much aware of the man who had shown him the way. "After kindling a fire," wrote Archibald Menzies, his surgeon and botanist, "and refreshing ourselves on whatever game and fish the day afforded, we drank a cheerful glass

Queen Charlotte Sound (Webber)
Captain Cook was on his third voyage when this picture of Queen Charlotte Sound was painted. The sound had become his base in New Zealand; he returned to it as a place increasingly familiar, setting up tents among Maoris who had learnt to accept his sailors and their "goblin" ship.

to the memory of Captain Cook, whose steps we were now pursuing. . . ." The ship's company was to find, and frankly admit, that his "delineations" had left little for them to finish.

Frenchmen came too: Marion du Fresne in 1772, only three years after the *Endeavour*, and staying too long in the Bay of Islands, until for unexplained reasons the Maoris killed him. Twenty-one years later Antoine de Bruni d'Entrecasteaux passed to the north on his way to the Kermadecs; and later still, in 1827, Dumont d'Urville began his long and patient survey of the New Zealand coast.

The French left names and an influence; and so also did sealers, British and American, making their discoveries for practical reasons, since they had to know where they were going along coasts that could be treacherous. It was an American, Owen F. Smith, who first sailed a ship through Foveaux Strait.

The convict settlement at New South Wales was founded in 1788. Victims of the harshest penal code in Europe were transported to a prison large enough to meet Britain's export requirements in crime and misery. New Zealand was too close to Australia to be left in isolation, and ships were soon crossing the Tasman. Some were sealers, eager for the killing before the harmless but useful creatures of rock and sea—sleek, brown-eyed and mournfully hoarse of voice—were clubbed almost to extinction. Others were traders in flax, or anything else that could be bought for a blanket

74

or musket—including, while the supply lasted, the heads of Maori chiefs, tattooed and smoked. Their captains found good anchorages, tested the bar at Hokianga, and by bold seamanship survived (with occasional losses) the perils of a coast which Captain Cook left with relief and was unwilling to see again.

Apart from sealers, who headed for the south, shipping from New South Wales came generally to harbours of the far north: the Bay of Islands, Whangaroa and Hokianga. Some of the earliest captains sailed confidently or foolishly into danger. Maoris were now seen at Port Jackson. They were men of fine physique, eager to learn new trades, and making good seamen. To the masters of ships, however, they were still savages, and could be treated roughly.

Captains had often been coarsened by years at sea, by a long habit of authority over tough and illiterate sailors. One such man was Captain Thompson of the *Boyd*, a vessel of 609 tonnes which in 1809 was taken by Maoris at Whangaroa. They still show you, at this northern harbour, where it all happened, though the scene is not easily recaptured from waters on which flotillas of launches, equipped for big-game fishing, now ride at anchor. And a tar-sealed road follows the foreshore where once, on a morning in early summer, excitement and death came to a native village.

This remains the best-known episode of its kind, symbolising intrusion and rejection as people of different races touched and clashed and drew sullenly apart. After many years there are still conflicting versions. A report widely accepted as the most authentic was written for the owner of the *Boyd* by a Sydney merchant, Alexander Berry. He was part-owner of a ship, the *City of Edinburgh*, which in December 1809 was loading spars at the Bay of Islands. News of the *Boyd* was brought to him by Maoris, and when loading was finished he set out with three armed boats on what he himself admitted was "a business of some danger". Bad weather drove him back, but a second attempt was successful. The burnt-out hull of the *Boyd* was found at the top of the harbour.

Berry was not only a brave man: he had tact and good sense, and was able to rescue four survivors, a woman, two young girls, and an apprentice. "I did all this by gentle measures, and you will admit that bloodshed and revenge would have answered no good purpose." The ship, he explained, had been taken on the third morning after her arrival. "The captain had been rather too hasty in resenting some slight theft." He also ordered from the ship a visiting chief who came to ask for bread. "The proud old savage (who had been a constant guest at the Governor's table at Port Jackson) was highly offended at this treatment, immediately left the cabin, and after stamping a few minutes on the deck, went into his canoe."

Tension was rising; but the sailors, sewing canvas or going about their normal duties, did not feel it. Nor did they suspect that more natives than usual had come aboard, or sense hostility as the newcomers silently watched them. The tension snapped with a shot on the beach, where the Captain and four sailors had landed after breakfast. It came from the Captain's own gun as Maoris attacked them, and it killed a child. On the *Boyd* the waiting Maoris rose, each beside his man and each with his *patu*, and in a few seconds most of the crew were dead. A few sailors escaped to the rigging, but had to come down at last, under promise of fair treatment, and were taken ashore to be killed.

A woman passenger, Mrs Ann Morley, used tears and frantic embraces to persuade a minor chief to spare her. She was taken to the beach with two girls (one of them her daughter), and would have been struck down there if women of the village had not rushed screaming to save her. To reach a canoe from the ship, she and the children had to walk on slippery decks, past bodies that were already being cut up for the ovens.

The apprentice, Thomas Davis, had escaped to the hold, where he stayed for three days, expecting any moment to be found and killed. When finally discovered, the tribesmen were sated, and he was allowed to live. The Second Mate was less fortunate. He begged for his life and managed to stay alive for a fortnight, after which he was clubbed and eaten. Seventy Europeans died in the massacre.

Berry's account was restrained; but he could not speak Maori, and he appears to have been mistaken in some details. He was also gentler with Captain Thompson than the facts required him to be, and perhaps wanted him to be exonerated. But he made one significant statement: "I think if the Captain had received Te Pahi (the visiting chief) with a little more civility, that he would have informed him of his danger. . . ."

The real reason for his danger was revealed five years later, when Samuel Marsden was at the scene of the tragedy. He talked to men who had taken part in it, questioning them closely. One of them, and perhaps the principal actor, was a chief named Tara, known to Europeans as "George". J. L. Nicholas, who was with Marsden at Whangaroa, disliked and feared George, and introduced him unfavourably to posterity in *Voyage to New Zealand* (1817): "His features were not unsightly, but they appeared to veil a dark and subtle malignity of intention, and the lurking treachery of a depraved heart was perfectly legible in every one of them."

Nicholas was responding emotionally, remembering details of the massacre and seeing what he expected to find, a savage and implacable killer. Marsden did not respond in the same way, though the taking of the *Boyd* had profoundly shocked him. He knew George, had entertained him at Parramatta, and was not dismayed or deceived by the "coarse familiarity of manner" which —according to Nicholas—he had acquired "from his intercourse with European sailors".

George had served on whalers, and spoke English fluently. He was one of two chiefs returning to New Zealand as sailors on the *Boyd*. George became ill and was unable to work, whereupon the master had him flogged, and threatened to throw him overboard. The sailors, taking their cue from the Captain, treated him after the manner of their kind, though perhaps more with rough humour than malice. But insult and injury were intolerable to George and to his people, inflamed by reports of what had been done to him. Even so, a massacre might have been averted if Captain Thompson had been able to receive with civility the chief who came aboard at Whangaroa.

Astrolabe in French Pass (de Sainson) (Detail only)
In the track of *Endeavour* and *Resolution* came the ships of famous navigators,
among them the *Astrolabe*, commanded by Dumont D'Urville. Its passage
through French Pass in 1827, depicted in this painting, was one of the great
feats of seamanship which helped to open the coasts for early travellers.

The death of 70 people was a heavy price for a lacerated back; but it was by no means the end of the story. In those days, when Maori and European were first trying to overcome differences in language and custom, the scope for misunderstanding was almost infinite. Marsden was told that the chief who had been ordered ashore was Te Puhi, not Te Pahi: the names sounded too much alike on European tongues, and were confused in earliest reports of the tragedy. Te Pahi had been at Whangaroa at the time, and was reputed to have tried to save some of the sailors. Whalers at the Bay of Islands, however, were convinced that he had led the attack on the *Boyd*. They came up in seven boats, landed before daybreak on Te Pahi's island in the Kerikeri River, and shot every man, woman and child they could find, including the chief himself.

This version of events was corroborated by Hongi and Ruatara. In accordance with *utu*, the death of Te Pahi required atonement; and tribes at the Bay of Islands sought it soon afterwards by declaring war—not against whalers, as European logic might have suggested, but against the people of Whangaroa. In this way the flogging of one man led in fatal sequence to two massacres and a chain of battles which continued—as *utu* thrived on new killings—until after the death of Hongi.

Ships avoided the Bay of Islands for several years; but gradually, as a few bold or desperate men began to arrive, and even to live among the New Zealanders, something was learnt of native law and custom. Europeans could not be expected to understand quickly the system of behaviour which governed the lives of these people: only the tribesmen, walking delicately outside their villages, and relaxed and good-tempered within them, could know what was *tika*, correct, or explain the all-pervading *tapu*.

Communication was so imperfect, when Maori met Pakeha, that murders and massacres reported from pre-colonial times now seem to have been remarkably few. Europeans who began to come ashore were unlikely to have been notable for intellect or sensitivity: many were unable to respond to natural courtesy, and could have mistaken it for weakness. But they were Pakeha, and even outcasts had to be treated carefully, since the Pakeha had their own form of *utu*, with ships and soldiers to support it, and were quick to take vengeance if harm were done to the lowest of their kind.

Whatever the reasons (and there must have been several, closely interlocked), the New Zealanders learnt to be patient. "I once saw with indignation," wrote Augustus Earle in 1828, "a chief absolutely knocked overboard from a whaler's deck by the ship's mate. Twenty years ago so gross an insult would have cost the lives of every individual on board the vessel; but, at the time this occurred, it was only made the subject of complaint, and finally became a cause of just remonstrance with the commander of the whaler." The natives were learning about Pakeha customs more quickly than the strangers were learning about theirs.

The massacre of the *Boyd* was an almost traumatic experience for both races. Marsden returned to it again and again in his journals, probing and explaining, and tracing its ramifications through years of tribal history. Seventeen years after the event it was still so much talked about that Augustus Earle felt impelled

Loading on Hokianga Harbour (Charles Heaphy)
At Horeke, 42 kilometres from the entrance to Hokianga Harbour, a Sydney
firm opened a shipyard in 1826; and here, 13 years later, Charles Heaphy found
tall ships loading spars cut from the kauri forest nearby. Many early travellers
passed this way.

to insert a full account of it in his book, using the text of Alexander
Berry's letter. European historians dwelt upon it one after another,
enlarging the story and correcting inaccuracies. Even today the
tragedy keeps its power, and leaves unanswered questions. We
would like to know more about the survivors. Mrs Morley died at
Lima, we are told; the two girls returned to Sydney, presumably
to conventional lives; and Thomas Davis went home to England.
And that is all.

They are not the only people of our early history whose stories
remain unfinished, or are hard to find. Men and women make
brief appearances and fade from view, like figures seen for an
instant at the end of a forest trail and believed afterwards to have
been phantoms. Charlotte Edgar was one of them. She consorted
with pirates when the brig *Venus* was seized (in 1806) by a
mutinous mate and a few convicts. It was a shabby and ineffectual
exploit, entirely lacking in the picturesque side of villainy.
Charlotte had an infant and was put ashore at Kororareka with a
second female, Catherine Hagerty.

Later, when the mate was captured and sent off to England,
and Catherine died, Charlotte refused the offer of a passage in
another ship. Her fate, says McNab, "is unknown". Charlotte and
Catherine are believed to have been the first white women to live

"Kororadika" Beach (Augustus Earle)
Augustus Earle's visit to Kororareka in 1827 produced the most interesting
passages in his book, *Narrative of a Nine Months' Residence in New Zealand*.
He found the beach "the general place of rendezvous for all Europeans whom
chance might bring into this bay".

in New Zealand, and only Charlotte lived long enough to be a settler. We can merely guess what happened to her as whalers came and went, or as she drifted out of sight in a Maori village. The beach was thinly settled in those days, and nobody cared.

There may have been other people, men and women, who landed from unknown or forgotten ships and disappeared without leaving a trace on legend or history. Who, for instance, was the slave encountered by Marsden at Kaipara in 1820? "On the sandhills," he wrote, "we met a young man about 24 years old, his complexion very fair, with light hair. His master was with him. I saw he was an European from his countenance and asked his master, who informed me his father was an European and he had got him originally from the Bay of Islands. I wished to redeem him with a view of sending him to the missionary settlement for instruction, but his master did not seem willing to part with him." An impression remains that this time Marsden did not try very hard; and we find ourselves wondering why.

These people belong to the half-light of our history; but there are others, individuals and groups, whose appearance in later times have no sequels. The voyage of the *Rosanna*, a ship used by the first New Zealand Company for an abortive colonising venture in 1825, has been mentioned often enough; but the Scots who stayed in this country, or returned to it from Sydney when Captain Herd abandoned his plans for a settlement, deserve to be better known than they are for their quiet persistence.

Augustus Earle came upon some of them near Hokianga, "busily employed in cutting timber, sawing planks, and making oars for the Sydney market". At Kororareka he saw another "respectable body of Scotch mechanics" from the *Rosanna*: "Their persevering industry as yet has been crowned with success. . . ." Earle praised them for their enterprise; they interfered with no one, he said, and managed successfully "without either requiring or receiving any assistance from home".

The Scots near Hokianga were shrewd as well as industrious. They were making oars only a short distance from a shipyard opened by a Sydney firm at Horeke, and no doubt were able to win opportunities and small contracts from its manager, Captain David Clark. Earle was delighted with the shipyard, which he saw as "a snug little colony of our own countrymen, comfortably settled and usefully employed in this savage and unexplored country". Ships were being loaded with spars; and a new vessel, built of kauri, was taking shape nearby.

This was at the head of the Hokianga, 42 kilometres from the harbour entrance. Charles Heaphy was there in 1839, and saw similar activity, with the scene not much altered. Tall ships were close inshore, loading kauri planks, and above them the hillsides were still dark with forest. Heaphy depicted the scene in one of his best-known paintings. The place is named Kahu-Kahu in some captions used for reproductions, but locals say that this identifies the terrace above the settlement. Maori place-names were used precisely to make every feature distinct from the surrounding landscape. The beach and adjoining flat land have always been known as Horeke.

Whalers in Port Otago (Le Breton)
Whalers had found New Zealand by the end of the 18th century, and in the
next few decades their ships dropped anchor in the harbours of both islands.
These ships were at Port Otago, with some of their sailors thankfully ashore,
a few years before the founding of Dunedin.

It was once the threshold of an area thickly settled, with villages
and large cultivations; but it did not grow, as some believed it
would, into a European town. The bar at the harbour mouth
became too serious a deterrent as ships grew bigger, and trade
moved southwards. Today the village at Horeke is a collection of
small houses, some on stilts above the tidal waters; and half the
population (of a few hundred only) are Pakehas. Most of the
Maoris have gone to Auckland. The hills around, which in the
times of Earle and Heaphy were dense forest from base to summit,
now have a secondary growth of low scrub, and there is talk of
reafforestation.

Augustus Earle stayed briefly in 1827, and then moved across
country with native guides. He was an artist who not only walked
the Maori trails, but *saw* them: "No other animal, except man,
ever traverses this country, and *his* track cannot be mistaken, since
none ever deviate from the beaten footpath, which was in

consequence in some places (where the soil was light) worn so deep as to resemble a gutter more than a road."

He was less reliable as an observer of human behaviour. Criticism of the missionaries was shown later to have been unfair, sharpened by resentment against their treatment of a friend, and perhaps of himself, for they did not approve of his "connexion with a native woman". Outcasts at the Bay of Islands were seen too much in black and white, especially the "Beach rangers". These men, he said, had been thrown off whalers for crimes that would have brought them to the gallows in England. Most had "gone native", and in Earle's opinion were giving the Maoris a poor impression of the British character.

Other men had fallen still lower—"a third class of our country-men . . . whose downcast and sneaking looks proclaim them to be runaway convicts from New South Wales". They were idle and vicious, Earle declared, "and much feared in the Bay of Islands". This may have been true of some, though fugitives were often men who had been transported for small offences. Frederick Maning was more tolerant when he wrote in *Old New Zealand* (1863) of ex-convicts as "that class who never could remember to a nicety how they had come into the country, or where they came from".

It is evident, however, that the various groups or classes under Earle's disapproving eye could only have been found in a growing community; and Kororareka was growing fast. From the beginning of the century, and perhaps earlier, whalers had found the Bay an ideal place to rest and refit after a year or two in the Pacific, cruising for sperm oil. No harbour dues had to be paid; the ships could anchor close to a beach; wood and fresh water were found nearby in abundance; and no magistrate could detain a sailor for breaking the peace. True, the natives were cannibals and needed watching; but they were eager to sell pork and potatoes for muskets and ironware, and the women were ready to entertain sea-weary men.

Sometimes the visitors stayed too long, or found the women too interesting, and inevitably there were "incidents". In 1830 Captain Brind, of the *Toward-Castle*, was the instigator of the so-called "Girls' War", a series of Ngapuhi expeditions against southern tribes. The amorous Brind took two women as his wives, and settled for a time on shore to enjoy the comforts of home life. But he was fickle as well as amorous: the wives were soon discarded and replaced by two others.

All four girls came together in a bathing party, splashing and laughing with every appearance of good humour. Unfortunately the banter touched delicate matters and grew into insult; and the mother of the first two girls, listening indignantly from the beach, ran into the water and attempted to drown their supplanters. The girls had good connections, and at first news of the incident their warriors rushed furiously to arms. Nearly a hundred people died in the battle that followed.

James Kemp, who saw results of the fighting, sent an angry report to the Church Missionary Society. "The South Sea whalers," he wrote, "are, by far the greatest part of them, great enemies to us and to the cause in which we are engaged, and

Queen Street, Auckland (Edward Ashworth)
The founding of Auckland, in 1840, drew men down from the Bay of Islands, and some of the town's first Europeans were pioneer-tradesmen. They helped to build houses and stores depicted here in Queen Street three years later.

Captain Brind is one of the worst. . . ." Another witness, Peter Bays, thought the Captain was blamed unfairly. In *The Wreck of the Minerva* (1831), he commented that "the natives were rather instigated to hostilities by laws of their own than provoked to it by any allurement which a foreigner might throw in their way". Bays had a good opinion of Brind, who had given him passage after the loss of his own ship, the *Minerva*, and treated him hospitably. But the Maoris, like the missionaries, continued to blame the captain of the *Toward-Castle*.

The congregation of whalers at the Bay led to a growth of European as well as native trade. Agents from New South Wales began to set themselves up in small houses along the beach at Kororareka, and grog-shops were opened by men able to deal in a knock-about way with thirsty sailors. One of them was John Poyner, believed to have been an escaped convict. He died in 1835 and was the first person to be buried in a cemetery at Kororareka. A booklet published in 1967 by the Christ Church Trust at Russell describes Poyner as "a notorious trouble-maker" who had opposed the purchase of land for a burial ground. "In the end, willy nilly, he contributed to the church programme, for the fee for his interment went into the building fund. His grave is not marked."

Whalers at Kororareka were blue-water men, coming to New Zealand for rest and refreshment, and sailing afterwards, high into the Pacific. Some came back, briefly, and left again; but for most

Whaling Station, Kapiti (J. A. Gilfillan)
Whalers came and went; but some began to stay, setting up shore stations. In 1839, when Edward Jerningham Wakefield visited this station on Kapiti, he found a tough breed of men with their own customs and code, and almost their own language. Wakefield saw them as the country's true pioneers.

of them the visits were interludes, to be replaced later by the delights of Sydney or Valparaiso. Life for these men was hard and precarious, and often short. Beaches of the north, and the dream-like shapes of offshore islands, swam before them as in a mirage, and were forgotten. Sometimes there was the memory of a woman, but that too would fade after the ship had dropped below a few more rims of ocean.

Some sailors, however, did not want to go. By 1830, shore-based whalers were beginning to set up their stations, usually with small resources. A ship was a large investment; but a man with a few sovereigns in his pocket could buy a longboat, some trypots, windlasses and barrels; and every sailor or ex-convict had a knife at his belt and another in his baggage. Instead of facing three years at sea in a whaler, a few men who knew their business could make a living by joining together and working five months of the year.

Right whales came down the west coast of the North Island and through Cook Strait to eastern waters of the South Island from

Mr Rhodes' Station (Sir Wm Fox)
Europeans who settled in Canterbury before the Pilgrims arrived included the Rhodes brothers. Two of them, George and Robert, were managing a property at Purau, bought from the Greenwoods in 1847. The brown hills of Banks Peninsula were already softened by pasture, spreading up from a lonely farmhouse.

May to October; and soon, from a point near New Plymouth to the farthest coasts of Otago and Southland, the longboats were setting out in pursuit. It was not necessary now for a man to leave his woman: she was at the settlement, learning to keep his house as clean and shipshape as a sailor expected it to be, bearing his children, and sometimes getting him safely home from too much grog and quarrelsome friends.

By 1844, when the industry had reached its peak, 32 well-found stations were operating 68 boats and employing 650 men. Smaller parties worked independently, and as many as 400 whales were taken in a good season. But the good times lasted only about 20 years. As fewer whales came through the strait, whaling grew intermittent and gradually ceased. A single station, placed strategically in Tory Channel, lasted until recent times.

The decades between 1830 and 1850 produced some of the most robust individuals in New Zealand history. An air of legend clings to them. The nature of their work, and their adventures, gave them large and even heroic proportions. Edward Jerningham Wakefield, who visited some of their stations in 1839, wrote of them with a certain awe. He sailed in a whaleboat with Jack Guard, famous for feats of strength and daring when he snatched his wife and child from captivity. And Guard moved among men of comparable stature. Stories were soon being told of Dicky Barrett around Cook Strait, of John Jones at Waikouaiti and southwards, and the Weller brothers in Otago Harbour.

The whalers had to meet hardship and danger when they first tried to set up shore stations. Natives were sometimes hostile, plundering stores and burning their small houses. Conditions improved as Maori women began to live with the newcomers, standing between their husbands and the tribes. Soon, too, Maoris were going out in the longboats as oarsmen, and later as harpooners. The settlements became orderly, though still disturbed by drunkenness and fighting in the idle times.

Some at least of the travelling men were beginning to stay ashore, facing hard times and danger just to be there. They may not always have known why they clung to this beautiful but barbarous land, since at first their earnings were meagre, and they were not men who planned for a future. Nor were they men who looked twice at a landscape, except to see what could be taken from it for food and timber. But something drew and held them, a taste of freedom, or a particular woman; and for a time at least they followed their trade, and then passed on through other occupations into the silences of history.

If their time at the shore stations had been longer, they might have left a deeper mark on New Zealand life, and especially its language. Edward Jerningham Wakefield went ashore at Kapiti, and found the whalers' *argot* unintelligible until it was translated. They had their own words for every article of trade, using them so that the Maoris would not be able to pick up their meanings when prices were discussed in their presence, just as some parents today use a private language above the heads of their children. Pigs were "grunters", blankets were "dust spreaders", and tobacco was "weed". A chief was a "nob", a slave became a "doctor", a woman was a "heifer", a girl a "titter", and a child a "squeaker". A few of their words crept into the vernacular and never quite left it; but most are gone, replaced now by slang imported from overseas, or picked up from disc jockeys, and in no way derived from or related to our life and work.

Wakefield saw the whalers as the first pioneers. Before our arrival, he wrote, "they had explored the coast and seaboard country, and had introduced new wants as well as new vices, and a considerable degree of respect for the physical qualities of the Pakeha among the aboriginal population. With the exception of the expedition made by Marsden in 1814, I believe that in every instance these rough pioneers had smoothed the way for a more valuable civilisation; and that the missionaries, or the settlers, followed on their traces."

Wakefield disliked missionaries (as indeed did most "Company" men), and was always ready to denigrate them. So also were

Lyttelton Immigration Barracks (Sir Wm Fox)
Immigration barracks—long and single-storeyed in this picture—awaited the
first settlers at Lyttelton. "The only fear with these," wrote Charlotte Godley
(whose own house nearby had six rooms) "is . . . that they will be too
comfortable, and tempt the emigrants to remain in them longer than is
necessary."

Augustus Earle and Charles Heaphy; and perhaps it was under-
standable that artists and men of the world should resent actions
and policies which, in their view, took away from the Maoris their
natural dignity and replaced it with habits and manners from those
areas of European life which artists most despised. There was,
however, some truth in Wakefield's judgment. The missionaries
had set up their bridgehead in the north; and the whalers set up
one of their own in middle and southern parts of the country. From
these two groups came strong elements of colonial life, persisting
to this day, and perhaps leaving a dichotomy in the national
character.

Yet the two kinds of outpost had similarities as well as sharp
differences. Missionary and whaler both had to live in isolation.
The missionaries were protected to a certain extent by their
vocation: a suggestion of *tapu* was placed around them by friendly
chiefs, and they were expected to be benefactors. Whalers lived
among the Maoris more or less on their own terms, relying on
courage and luck and physical strength. The missionaries also had
courage, but their strength was in patience and fortitude, and
lacked the physical attributes which Maoris most admired.

In both situations the group could survive only by staying cohesive, by closing itself against darkness or savagery outside. The missionaries wavered and almost failed as their group was divided by friction and individual backsliding. Whaling settlements were in danger of collapse if their members fought too long or too often among themselves. Yet in their own way they were introducing a rule of law, even though at first it was only the "law of the bay". They had codes of behaviour, and rules and penalties, and accepted a discipline imposed by their leaders or by common decision.

The cohesion of the group, whether with missionaries or whalers, was at first a condition of survival. It was also the result of a democratic process which was to be strengthened by the arrival of settlers. In a "new" country, where settlements were enclaves in what seemed to be an encircling wilderness, democracy meant security, and had to be as close as possible to its true form, a common will that could be exercised through open debate, and in an assembly small enough to allow all men to speak their opinions.

This may help to explain much in our history that now seems to have been timid and colourless, with mediocrity prevailing because men wanted to be safe. But ours is a very short history, and it may be too soon to speak of a national character as if its components were fixed and unchangeable. If there has been too much thought of security, it may be because the impulse came first from men who lived dangerously, leaving a splash of colour which may have kept some quality of renewal that will begin to show itself when the times are suitable.

In the South Island the whalers were pioneers in an immediate and physical sense as they built their huts and set up trypots at the edge of a large and empty country. Until their arrival, at Otakau in 1832, at Peraki, Waikouaiti and Jacobs River in 1837, and in the next few years at adjacent sites, the South Island was without settlers and almost without inhabitants. The Maori population had been small since the passing of the moa-hunters, and had been nearly wiped out by Te Rauparaha's raids between 1828 and 1831.

The raids from Kapiti were over, and there was no more fighting, or danger of it, when whalers began to work from shore stations, and the first settlers looked around for land. The history of Canterbury and Otago has therefore been touched with comparative lightness by the Maori. Isolated events are remembered, but have had little impact on the European imagination. The siege of Kaiapoi, which ended with the virtual extinction of the Ngai Tahu, took place in 1831, only 19 years before the arrival of the Canterbury Pilgrims; but it seemed from the beginning to be a story from antiquity, in no way touching the life of the settlement.

If interest depended on European involvement, it should have been supplied by Te Rauparaha's version of a wooden horse. In this case the "horse" was a schooner, the *Elizabeth*. Its captain, the infamous Stewart, allowed Te Rauparaha and a band of Ngati Toa to conceal themselves in the ship on a voyage to Akaroa; and when tribesmen came unsuspectingly to the beach at Wainui they were surprised and killed, and their chief was taken to Kapiti for a more ceremonial death. Few episodes in New Zealand history have stronger elements of drama and tragedy, but it stays little noticed

Mangles Grass Valley (Sir Wm Fox)
The first Europeans to see this West Coast landscape were Thomas Brunner,
William Fox and Charles Heaphy. In 1846, on Brunner's first journey to the
Buller, they paused by the Teraumai River, entering a solitude still primeval.

in old books, whereas the story of James McKenzie, a drover who
stole sheep in 1855, left his name on the map, and became a sort
of folk-hero in modern fiction.

Te Rauparaha did not go beyond Rakaia on his southern
forays, and the ravaged camp-sites were fading into landscape when
the colonists came. This immunity from warfare had its effect on
a nascent literature. It appeared sometimes as if North and South
Island writers of an earlier period were writing from different
countries. There were good reasons for differences of outlook.
Thirty years before the first of the Four Ships anchored in
Lyttelton Harbour, the beach at Kororareka was notorious
throughout the Pacific as a resort of sailors, a village of the roughest
sort, with grog shops and prostitutes. And throughout the north
a mingling of Maori and Pakeha was taking place, interrupted by
violence and inter-tribal fighting, but leaving a social ferment
which was helping to shape the country's future.

Northern writers of later times had all this at their backs, and
must have felt its power. They were aware of people, and especially
Maori people, to an extent unknown in the south. It can be no
accident of literature that the strongest vein in fiction, producing
some of our best novels, has emerged from the clash of two
cultures, and is being strengthened now by Maoris themselves,
bringing new insights and a hopeful vitality in the use of words.

Yet South Island writing had its own themes and incentives.
Their poets and writers responded first to solitude and the virgin

Hokitika River (after Barraud)
For many years, until roads and railways offered safe travel, a journey from
Canterbury to Westland was an expedition; but wandering men were drawn to
the mountains, and in the 1860s they were joined by gold seekers. Journey's
end was in sight when they paused here, by the Hokitika River.

hills. "A new country," wrote T. Cholmondeley, author of
Ultima Thule (1854) and one of the earliest Canterbury settlers,
"ought to produce new thoughts." It is easy to believe, in a
mountain silence, that new thoughts are possible. But solitude is
hard to bear, and brings inevitably a return to human warmth.
Charles Brasch's *The Land and the People* (1939) expressed the
need of a generation: "There are no dead in this land,/No personal
sweetness in its earth. . . ." The sentiment would have brought no
echo from battlefields and ruined *pas* in the north; but it was true
of its time and place, among the hills of Otago and Canterbury.

Whalers in the south had behind them a hinterland of hills
and gorges, rapid and tumultous rivers, and higher up the lakes
and huge white mountains. All this country was unknown, except
for what could be learnt from wandering Maoris. A few Britons
came down after 1840 from Wellington and Nelson, and the first
farms were taken up on the hills around Port Cooper and on the

92

Coromandel (Charles Heaphy)
In 1852, when gold was found at Coromandel, chiefs of the Ngati Maru tribe attended a meeting at Pata Pata to sign an agreement which opened tribal land for mining. The goldfield was disappointing, but Maoris had learnt a new and strange reason for land hunger.

adjacent plains. The "pre-Adamites", a somewhat pretentious name for a handful of squatters who arrived late in history, were scattered thinly around when Canterbury was founded in 1850. And surveyors were beginning to explore the interior.

There was much unknown territory. Ancient Maori trails had been forgotten, and the Southern Alps raised formidable barriers along the borders of Nelson and Canterbury. They were overcome by Thomas Brunner, a young surveyor who in 1846 completed a great achievement in exploration. A first journey, in the company of William Fox and Charles Heaphy, was made to Lake Rotoiti and down the Mangles River to the Buller. His companions were Maoris when later he went down the valleys of the Buller and the Grey, afterwards pushing 80 kilometres south of Okarito. The hardships endured by Brunner and his party gave this journey an epic quality unmatched by any other in New Zealand history. The travels of Captain W. Mein Smith and Frederick Tuckett, and a mixed company of other surveyors, and a few scientists, were less dramatic, but increasingly useful.

After the explorers came the wanderers. There was an early movement of young men from town to country, from station to station, and sometimes across the ranges in journeys undertaken with no purpose except to satisfy restless feet and a longing for the unattainable. Charles Money, who wrote a book typical of his period, *Knocking About in New Zealand* (1871), carried a swag through harsh country until he could look down on the Teremakau River, "which stole like the silver tresses of some ancient dame over its time-worn bed". The dame proved to be livelier than she looked when Charles camped later near her banks, and was nearly lost in one of her sudden floods.

Money and a friend were making for Westland to try their luck at the diggings; but they were half-hearted gold seekers, and achieved nothing. Yet something stays in his artless book which suggests that this young man, and others like him, had felt the power and strange attraction of the bush, and would never be entirely happy outside it. They knew it in the spacious and quiet times, when trails were soon lost above the valleys, and an immense and brooding silence was threaded only by sounds of running water and the signals of birds. It offered nothing to men except its own presence; and in those days there was not the need of silence, or of separation from crowds and machines, that men would feel in the 20th century. Something had survived in it, from primeval silence, which drew men back, not for the sake of the journey, or for what lay beyond it, but to some source of power or renewal that could not be named or understood.

Money had already seen the goldfields of Otago, and was at Gabriel's Gully while the fever was at its worst. He had an eye for detail: "The town was surrounded by a vast net-work of holes of every shape and size, with heaps of variously coloured gravel beside them, stretching away as far as the eye could reach, till they were hidden by the turn of the valley." At the centre of the gully he found "canvas and galvanised iron stores, public-houses, restaurants, shanties of all descriptions and with every conceivable name, scattered around in all directions; while advertisements of nigger minstrels, gold buyers' prices, and placards, were flaunting everywhere".

The shanties and the pubs and dance halls would eventually be swept away, like rubbish carried on a rush of yellow water from the gorges; but the holes remained throughout the diggings in Otago, and would later be deepened or widened by Chinese fossickers, or a later generation of seekers. And so it was also on the West Coast, where by 1865 more than 7,000 men were looking for gold. Two years later the same men, or large numbers of them, had moved on to Coromandel; but here, where quartz claims could only be worked by battery, they had to form groups and small companies; and soon, inevitably, the big boys moved in.

The gold rushes brought men to the country who could be seen only as intruders. Unlike the settlers, they had nothing to give, but

Lake Manapouri (W. G. Baker)
Europeans first saw Manapouri in 1852. The few people able to reach it
100 years ago could not have foreseen that the lake would become the centre
of a famous debate, symbolising a new conflict between economic and ecological
needs.

were takers and spoilers. Although farmers were heavy-handed in
the early days, eager to exploit a rich soil, they learnt to live with
the land and to respect its needs and moods. The miners respected
only their own rights.

They came in thousands from Australia, and even from
California; and everywhere, at a rumour of more gold, they packed
their swags and moved on. Behind them were ruined valleys,
pitted with holes, their subsoil washed away in creeks and rivers.
Some of these men stayed in New Zealand, and were to become
good settlers; but the majority passed on, carrying their swags and
hopes up the gangways of ships bound for new and better diggings.

There is another side of this particular story. Miners in Otago
lifted the population in a few months from 13,000 to 30,000, a
huge increase at that time, and a profitable one. Dunedin's citizens
(or those who stayed at home, the "old identities") were unhappy
about the influx of strangers, the "new iniquity", but began to do
very well in business. The demand for tools and machines led to
the founding of Dunedin's heavy industries.

The conflict of interest or value in this situation became more familiar to New Zealanders in the second half of the 20th century. In the 1860s there was little time to think about it, and the country was still so large (or seemed to be) that only a few curmudgeons and nonconformists could see cause for uneasiness or complaint. It was impossible to have progress without change and some disruption. Everybody wanted to make money, and although change might appear to have been drastic in a spoiled valley there was good land left for farming. And in the meantime £25 million had come in from Otago goldfields.

Less enthusiasm was shown as gold became harder to find; and in 1886, when the first bucket dredge was built, a few people began to ask if this violent assault should be allowed to continue. As late as 1903, however, 201 dredges were at work in Otago and Southland, mostly along the Clutha and its tributary, the Kawerau. And in Westland the dredging has never really ceased, though gradually, as river valleys became hideous and sterile, with stones piled like cairns to commemorate the dead, it was restricted to areas where (it is said) the terrain has no promise of productive use.

The 19th century was by no means 100 years of unhindered progress; but it saw the arrival of forerunners, men and women who would show what could be done on the land or in isolated places, and whose effort and fortitude would set standards of behaviour that their descendants (for a generation or two, while colonial attitudes persisted) would respect and value.

For better or worse, but ineluctably, the long isolation of the Maoris was ended, and a process of nation-building brought strain and tension, sometimes creative, as the Europeans became a dominant majority. From those years emerged in outline or in embryo the situations and problems that challenge the nation today. They seem less strange, and less alarming, when old books and pictures help us to see how they all began.

Kaiwharawhara Mill (S. C. Brees)
Forest around Wellington was heaviest in the Hutt Valley, at Kaiwharawhara, and in Karori. One of the earliest sawmills was at Kaiwharawhara, a district on the road to Petone. Timber milled here was taken by bullock wagons to the growing settlements at Thorndon and Te Aro.

East from Ponsonby (Sam Stuart)
Ships were reaching the Waitemata before Auckland was founded, and harbour traffic grew rapidly with the new settlement. In 1877, when Sam Stuart painted this watercolour on a blue day, he could see a forest of masts outside the town.

Maori songs "from the tops of the *whare* or huts where they sat tying the rafters and thatch together with flaxen bands".

Further up the valley, on the banks of the Waiwhetu, he found squatters "no less busy and merry". His father in England, Edward Gibbon Wakefield, would have been gratified by the evidence of a democratic spirit operating with a necessary decorum. Masters and labourers worked together. Each "gentleman" had a retinue of workers from his own part of Britain: "Cornish miners and agricultural labourers had pitched their tents near Mr Molesworth; Kentish men dwelt near Mr George Duppa . . .; and many of the Scotch emigrants were collected . . . where Mr Dudley Sinclair and Mr Barton were erecting their dwellings."

Children nearby were "ruddy" and "flaxen-haired", straight out of a poem by Wordsworth. The natives, unaware that they were watching the arrival of Utopia, came with pork and potatoes to a ready-made market, and often stayed to help. But everybody knew his place, and the social decencies were observed as far as possible in the circumstances. A "capitalist" in a tent ate a meal in shirt-sleeves and drank his beer or wine from "excellent glass and crockery, with a clean table-cloth, a cruet-stand, and all the paraphernalia"; and outside, by a gipsy fire, his labourer had "an equally comfortable dinner", though at a proper distance, and without the tablecloth and glassware. The weather was as mild

Nelson (F. D. Bell)
As in Wellington, settlers at Nelson faced a shortage of land suitable for farming; but they were also more isolated, building their homes under hills which seemed for a time to enclose them too securely.

as a benediction, helping to give "the extensive bivouac the air of a picnic on a large scale. . . ."

The climate, indeed, was remarkable: nothing better, surely, could have been found outside the Garden of Eden. Newcomers were sometimes wet after crossing streams, or from "occasional showers of rain"; but "no one felt any injury to his health". Charles Heaphy, who had been Wakefield's shipmate on the *Tory*, was even more sanguine. The climate, he wrote later in *Narrative of a Residence in Various Parts of New Zealand* (1842), "is extremely equable, and, consequently, well adapted to persons suffering from, or dreading, pulmonary disease; and to whom the sudden change from extremes of warm and cold temperature is fatally injurious".

He could not deny that "some parts of the New Zealand coast are especially subject to heavy winds"; but he denied, almost with indignation, that wind at Port Nicholson could do "material injury" to a field of corn. Nevertheless, he added (good sense prevailing), a settler would be prudent "for several seasons, when clearing land, to leave a belt of forest round his section. . . ."

Apart from some slight "material damage", there was nothing to fear: the wind came and went, and left behind it "extraordinary salubrity". Without it, indeed, the effects of the sun on "the perpetually decomposing mass of vegetation under the New Zealand forest" would probably make the climate "as injurious as that of Java or Sierra Leone". And finally, triumphantly, Heaphy quoted a physician on an emigrant ship who said, after his first encounter with a gale in Wellington, that "the wind would oblige him to leave the country, as his business would there be nearly useless".

The climate since then has generally been described as bracing rather than salubrious. Bishop Selwyn, a Christian who almost certainly delighted in cold baths, summed it up succinctly: "No one can speak of the healthfulness of New Zealand till he has been ventilated by the restless breezes of Port Nicholson. . . ." He saw it as a good place to work in: "Active habits of industry and enterprise are evidently favoured by the elastic tone and perpetual motion of the atmosphere."

Settlers at Petone and in the Hutt Valley soon learnt what the weather could do to them. The picnic atmosphere was dispersed by "a brisk northerly wind", by rain which continued from the 23rd to the 27th of February, and on the first of March a south-east gale. Settlers were thus introduced to a meteorological sequence which successive generations have studied with interest, disbelief, and sometimes despair.

Wakefield and Heaphy were servants of the New Zealand Company, and wanted everything to be satisfactory, if not perfect. On his beach walk at Petone, and his excursion up the valley, Wakefield undoubtedly saw good humour and the camaraderie which men feel when they are thrown together on a big or testing occasion. But he also saw what he wanted to see, generalising freely and hopefully, and welcoming already the fulfilment of his father's dream.

He saw with approval the man of substance (soon to be a man of property) attended by faithful servants. As in England, the divisions of class and money would be preserved; but in this free-moving air the divisions would be maintained liberally by master, and accepted without servility by the man. The natives were cheerfully taking a place lower still. Everywhere was the suggestion of a little England, nascent in a settlement that was to be founded on land amply available, sold at a sufficient price, and worked by men who would be content with their station until by effort and thrift they could rise above it to prosperity and even affluence. How could Wakefield have known that the winds of change would blow as briskly as the winds of Wellington?

Already, as colonists landed and pitched their tents, an element of insecurity was weakening the first euphoria. These people had left England without knowing where they were going, except vaguely to New Zealand. They were on their way before land had been bought from the Maoris by Colonel William Wakefield's advance party, and indeed before the Company could be sure that land titles gained in this way would be acceptable to a colonial government after annexation to the Crown.

The *Aurora*, first of the emigrant ships, was somewhere at sea when Captain Hobson received his instructions; and settlers were at Port Nicholson several weeks before the Lieutenant-Governor arrived at Russell. It was all an adventure, perhaps; but it was imposed on men with families, and often without money, whose

New Plymouth (F. D. Bell)
Leading colonists were often artists, revealing a breadth of interest which later disappeared from public life. One of them was Francis Dillon Bell, Company agent at New Plymouth in 1847-48. In this picture he caught the loneliness of the settlement against Mount Egmont, a shape still alien to English eyes.

only wishes were a patch of good earth and steady employment. From the beginning there were doubts about the possession of land; and the few sites that could be chosen, although beautiful, were not always what had been promised by Company agents.

Apart from the Hutt Valley, where settlement was impeded by a river which flooded, very little land was suitable for farming. There was forest at Karori and Kaiwharawhara, and axes were soon to be heard at its margins; but hillsides above the valleys were steep and inhospitable, and beyond them the ranges closed in upon the harbour like walls, denying access to land that was rumoured to be open and fertile. The Maoris were not anxious to show the way. After the first excitements, and as ships kept coming, they began to complain of too many Pakehas. Was the whole tribe (they were heard to ask) coming from England to live in Petone? The sale of land became harder to negotiate, even before the proclamation of British sovereignty clouded the whole question of ownership.

Settlers began to feel again the anxieties they had hoped to leave behind in Britain. They had different causes, but followed a familiar pathway along the nerves. British people had come a long way to a country which kept an early-morning freshness; but another and older part of the world had come with them, and new difficulties were arising while every smallest part of household management was a continued improvisation.

103

Emigration had started, however, and could not now be stopped. In the next few years settlement was extended throughout the central districts. Colonists were landed at Nelson and New Plymouth, and a small number were diverted from Port Nicholson to a beach-head at Wanganui. In all these places the hopeful beginning, enlarged in spirit by a release from small and crowded ships after months at sea, was followed by doubt and disappointment, and then—as optimism returned—by a steady acceptance of life as it had to be lived in an isolated colony.

New Plymouth, like Wellington, was short of good land. It also needed a harbour, an artificial one that required money and labour beyond the colony's resources; and the Maoris were denying access and title to the interior. In spite of a good beginning, tensions began to build towards the showdown which Maoris now describe, with good reason, as the Land Wars of Taranaki.

At Nelson the newcomers found themselves among landscapes of surpassing beauty; but here too was trouble over land, leading to an early clash with the Maoris, and a harbour which frustrated all hopes of expansion as a commercial centre. Disappointment was sharpened for those who knew that the site was a second choice, accepted with misgivings. Nelson was to have been situated at Banks Peninsula; but the site was outside the limits of territory bought by Colonel Wakefield, and the proposal for a settlement at Port Cooper was vetoed by the Governor, anxious to keep new colonies as close as possible to his own headquarters.

Captain Hobson had set himself up in Russell, and seemed to indicate, by purchasing land for a house at a surprisingly high price, an intention to stay there. But Russell was another name for Kororareka, a place of ill repute; and once again the urge to make a new beginning, always strong in a country with clean landscapes, became irresistible. It was also, in Hobson's case, a temptation to which he was wise to succumb. His mission was mainly to protect the Maoris and to pre-empt all land to the Crown; and for these tasks he needed a more central position. He found it ideally at the Tamaki Isthmus, a neck of land between Waitemata and Manukau, sprinkled with volcanic cones, and the scene of historic battles between tribes whose opinion of the area had been as favourable as his own.

News of this decision was received at Port Nicholson with dismay and indignation. Settlers had hoped that their own town would become the centre of government, and perhaps had been encouraged in their hope by leaders or agents of the New Zealand Company whose position would have been strengthened by official acceptance of their *fait accompli*. The case for Port Nicholson had been advanced with a logic which was felt to be irrefutable by Samuel Revans, editor of the *Britannia Spectator*, and by most of his readers.

If the Governor wanted "centrality", what could be more central than a town on Cook Strait, at the bottom of one island and boldly facing another? If his mission was to govern, must there not be a population to be governed? Could he in all conscience be satisfied with a handful of traders and officials, and 32 artisans and their families who (it was faithfully reported) had come down with him from Russell in the *Anna Watson*?

Motueka Valley (after A. Campbell)
Not far from Nelson, in the Motueka Valley, a second settlement was founded
in 1842. The soil was ideal for small farms, and was to produce most of the
country's hops and tobacco. In these surroundings the countryside soon had
new shades of green under hillside forest.

True, Maoris were living at Tamaki, and Australians had been
arriving since the earliest rumour of settlement, hoping to buy land
for a few shillings an acre and sell it almost at once for a price 10
times higher; but these were scarcely to be seen as founders. At Port
Nicholson, on the contrary, were 1,500 Britons of good character
and with improving prospects. After the first landing at Petone a
more suitable town site had been found at Thorndon, fronting
deep water and sheltered anchorages in Lambton Harbour, and
houses were being built on flat land along and above the foreshore.
The fine harbour and central position made Port Nicholson a
proper choice, especially since everybody knew that settlement
in the Middle Island could be delayed but not prevented.

Hobson, however, had a different meaning for centrality. He
wanted to be placed between tribes which had been decimated by
recent warfare. More important, perhaps, was his need to stand
between the Maoris and land-hungry Europeans; and he could
best do this where the Maori population was thickest, from the
Waikato to the higher north. Hobson was intent upon his
immediate task, and had neither time nor inclination for the
Company's vision of a country sprinkled with smiling British
settlements. The Treaty of Waitangi had been signed, and Hobson

was trying conscientiously to carry out the responsibilities it had placed upon the Crown and its servant.

His preference for Auckland appeared to be the principal source of bad feeling between settlers and the government; but the real cause lay deeper, in a nagging insecurity at Port Nicholson. The New Zealand Company had acted quickly and boldly in sending emigrants without an official blessing; its aim was to set up a colony before British annexation, which then appeared to be imminent, and to a certain extent the policy succeeded. Simply by being there, the settlers had a claim to occupancy, especially in a country which for a long time would be thinly policed; and although their land tenure could be questioned and restricted, it could not in common justice be destroyed.

Yet the colonists were in great need of reassurance. The holiday mood had long disappeared among sharp reminders that life had to go on, and that life everywhere was precarious. Soon after Hobson's arrival at Russell and before his decision to move to Auckland, the settlers at Port Nicholson had to face alarms and calamity. A boy died from a spear wound; a row of labourers' huts was burnt to the ground; the entire settlement was shaken by an earthquake; and nine people were drowned off Petone when a boat overturned in a southerly gale.

New ships were arriving, and the main township at Thorndon was growing fast—a collection of huts and houses, apparently set down at random, but with streets and a few shops. There was still a shortage of land, much dissatisfaction with the slowness of Company surveyors, and uncertainty about the interior; and men with funds could find few openings except in trade. The obvious need was land, and more land, and a sound tenure while hills and valleys were converted into farms.

Then came alarming news from Sydney. A New Zealand Land Bill, passed by the Legislative Council of New South Wales, had declared all titles not derived from the Crown to be null and void. True, a Board of Commissioners would examine all claims, and was to be guided by "the real justice and good conscience of the case"; but the Bill also forbade any grant of land exceeding 1,036 hectares, or including natural features useful in defence, or any land suitable for a town site.

The inhabitants of Port Nicholson were stricken. They believed themselves to be in danger of losing "the very site of a town under their feet, which was at that moment being distributed to them for occupation and improvement". Ten days later, after rumour and wild speculation had done its work, people were seriously considering a general re-emigration to Chile.

Into this situation came a calming influence in the person of Dicky Barrett. The ex-whaler had set himself up, with a retinue of both races, in a clay-walled house in Thorndon; and his hospitality was a legend in the town. From the waterfront nearby could be seen an old cutter of 50 tonnes, built long ago at Queen Charlotte Sound, and now sitting on Lambton Harbour with a broom tied derisively to her masthead. Barret had some bills printed, announcing that the ship would soon be sailing for Valparaiso with "a high poop and experienced surgeon". In the

106

Paekakariki (John Gully)
Early travellers from the Manawatu came to this hillside road at Paekakariki
after driving along the beach from Waikanae. Before them lay a stiff climb,
the descent to Pahauatanui, and a road through forest which brought them to
hills above Kaiwharawhara and a breath-taking view of Wellington.

opinion of Edward Jerningham Wakefield, who was there when it
happened, this "squib" did more than anything else to end
proposals for another migration.

Dicky Barrett had learned long ago that things were seldom
as bad as they seemed; and his judgment was supported when
Colonel Wakefield returned from a visit to the Governor, and
confirmed later as—in due process of law—colonists were granted
titles to land bought in good faith and on reasonable terms. For a
time at least, the settlers put aside their fears. They were, however,
vulnerable to rumour. Impassable country lay between themselves
and the seat of government: news from the north came slowly by
ship, sometimes via Sydney, and could suffer a sea-change on the
voyage.

They were subject briefly to the laws of New South Wales, and
were startled by their severity. Jerningham Wakefield learnt with
surprise and alarm that he had become liable to seven years'
transportation by shooting a pig which was eating his potatoes, and
hastened to appease the owner with a pound. Much resentment
was felt at the appearance in Thorndon of "mounted" police,
trained in New South Wales to capture bushrangers, and now
using a boat instead of horses to bring a few prisoners from Petone
to a brand new gaol in Thorndon.

These were temporary grievances, soon to disappear as New
Zealand ceased to be governed from Sydney. Yet the proclamation

of British sovereignty brought new irritations, and a trial of strength between a governor with full authority and small resources, and men at Port Nicholson with no authority in law, outside Company regulations, but a *de facto* leadership.

The colonists had set up their own council, with Colonel Wakefield as President, and from the arrival of the *Aurora* had attempted to introduce the rule of law. Wakefield and his council had no power except by the vote of settlers, although it could be argued that they were justified by isolation, and were in fact a community simply trying to stay British. After the declaration of British sovereignty, however, the council took a step which seemed to go beyond its rather tenuous mandate.

Colonel Wakefield expected all settlers to carry arms in an emergency, and he now called upon males aged between 18 and 60 to form themselves into a militia under his command. His nephew, Edward Jerningham, wrote later as if this measure had been approved, by Maoris as well as Pakehas; but Edward was invariably an apologist for his uncle, and for the Company he represented. It is unlikely that this first and premature experiment in conscription was received without dissent. There may well have been substance in a rumour from the Bay of Islands that a ship's captain and his passengers had described the colonists at Port Nicholson as "a turbulent set of rebels who were establishing a republic".

The Governor probably had other sources of information, and knew what had to be done. Lieutenant Willoughby Shortland, the Colonial Secretary, came down to Britannia with 30 soldiers and some mounted police (without their horses); and with due ceremony the Union Jack was hoisted, and the Queen of England's sovereignty proclaimed. Shortland has been described by some of his contemporaries as a pompous and tactless person, and he was criticised for the speed with which he dissolved the settlers' council. It may well be that he enjoyed the task rather more than was necessary; but he was acting under orders, and the orders seem to have been justified in the circumstances.

This was the end of self-rule by settlements; but it was by no means the end of independence, or of an attempt to make it a political reality. Friction between Wellington and Auckland was in those days a friction between settlers and governor, and it continued and developed after Hobson died and was succeeded by FitzRoy and—in 1846—by George Grey. The colonists had had a taste of freedom, and only self-government, for the country as a whole, would now satisfy them.

They appeared to have won it in 1846, when representative government was conferred on New Zealand by Act of Parliament; but Grey was able to prevent or delay its full operation. The country was divided into two provinces, with a lieutenant-governor in charge of the southern part, New Munster (a name which, like Britannia for Wellington, and Petre for Wanganui, was soon mercifully abandoned); and a semblance of self-rule was provided through two provincial councils.

The councils were unworkable. Colonists wanted nothing less than a central government, with a fully elected house; and in the end they got it. There would still be years of uneasy compromise

Mercer (Alfred Sharpe)
New towns did not always fulfil their early promise. Mercer was growing fast in
in the 1860s, when travellers disembarked from river steamers to join the
Auckland coach. But new roads diverted the traffic; and today Mercer remains
a small town through which express trains pass without stopping.

between a "general" government and the provinces, increased to
six by the Constitution Act of 1852, and administered by elected
councils and superintendents. But the aim was defined from the
beginning; and the first big step, to parliamentary government,
was taken in 14 years. Only the facts of geography prevented an
earlier success.

Auckland showed less enthusiasm than Wellington for the
movement towards independence, partly because it had become the
seat of government. The consuming interest around the isthmus
was trade: it could be said that Aucklanders were too busy to be
doctrinaire, and that the rapid growth of their town and province
gave them substance instead of argument. It might even be claimed
that their climate favoured a more relaxed approach to politics.
Certainly it was milder than in Wellington, in spite of occasional
cloudbursts.

The winds which swept through Cook Strait may have been
invigorating, but by too much repetition they could make men
irritable. A degree of irritation is perhaps an indispensable element
of politics. It may also be worth mentioning, as a fact of history,

that the man still revered in Auckland as the city's "Father" (John Logan Campbell) was highly successful in trade, whereas Wellington had several Fathers, preserved in effigy on pedestals around Parliament and in Bolton Street cemetery (or what is left of it), and all of them were politicians.

Although there were sharp differences between Auckland and Wellington, the two settlements had similar problems, especially in the earliest decades. Auckland was short of good farmland, and had to stay short while Maori rights were being protected. Wellington also needed suitable land; surveyors were soon looking beyond its coastal ranges to the broad valley of the Wairarapa, and to country hidden beneath forest in the Manawatu, though here also the Maoris were now unwilling to sell.

Men who wanted to make money in the main settlements had to set themselves up as traders. Both towns depended heavily on capital from Britain, and neither had enough of it. The Governor's revenue was meagre; and although it was improved by the sale of land, it remained inadequate. Money was brought in from Australia, and with it came businessmen, looking for opportunity and quick profits.

In Wellington the New Zealand Company was using the money of British shareholders to fill warehouses with foodstuffs, household goods and implements, and also to build a few roads. One road followed the western side of the harbour to the Hutt Valley, and was described by admiring visitors as "an ornament to the colony". Another, from Kaiwharawhara to Porirua, was merely a bridle track, 1.5 metres wide; but it gave access to the Kenepuru valley, and followed a stream with the same name through 25 kilometres of "bush". Men who rode to a whaling station at Porirua, or onwards to Wanganui (where an outlet was being sought for immigrants who could not find land at Port Nicholson), valued the track for practical reasons; but some of them may have paused once or twice to become aware of the forest, and perhaps to shrug it from them as their horses' hoofs once again broke the disconcerting silence.

If today they could pass that way they would see factories near a ruined stream, with industrial debris on its banks, and above them long streets of houses on terraced hillsides. Near the line of the track is an electrified railway and a road which carries a stream of vehicles beyond the suburbs. Miraculously, there are still birds, mainly of the adaptable kind brought in from England; but the birds which were heard in the 1840s have long vanished from those parts. Yet only two persons, each living about 65 years, would be needed to cross a time-bridge from track to motorway, from horse to electric train, and from forest silence to an endless sound of traffic, louder but harsher than surf on a beach.

Wellington was helped in its formative years by Company money and enterprise; but private capital was large enough to arouse the interest of Sydney merchants: the necessities of life, and some of its luxuries, were soon crossing the Tasman to warehouses, shops and hotels along the edge of Lambton Harbour. Charles Heaphy mentioned the names of 17 merchants (including some of the original settlers from Britain) who had built substantial warehouses before the end of 1841.

The Spit, Napier (Barraud)
Napier was once administered from Wellington, but broke away—an action much approved in Auckland. As the outlet for some of the best sheep country in the North Island, it was becoming an important trading centre when this view of the Spit was drawn in 1860.

The settlers provided their own market at first, living on capital; but gradually, as farm produce came in for local use and for export to New South Wales, and ships brought more settlers and injections of new capital, a momentum was gained which promised to grow indefinitely. Even the ships which brought immigrants and cargoes helped the movement of trade, since they had to be provisioned at the end of the voyage. From the arrival of the *Tory* until November 1841, Lambton Harbour received 340 ships with an aggregate burden of 55,421 tonnes.

All this trading was helpful, and would later be valuable; but it was being created and stimulated too much by savings from outside, and not enough by "new" money earned on the spot. This truth came suddenly into the open when the country had the first of a long series of depressions. As early as 1845 the settlers had to learn that progress was illusory unless it grew from a production, especially agricultural, which served a true and continuing demand at home and abroad.

In the meantime Wellington and Auckland watched each other from a distance. Settlers at both ends of the island were quick to suspect injury or harmful intention, and the colonial press became loud with protest and vilification. The Government needed labour to build houses and roads in Auckland, and tried to entice workers from Wellington. It failed for a good reason: the wages offered were not high enough. In spite of labour shortages, however, Auckland was growing fast, and grew faster still as boatloads of emigrants arrived from Scotland and England.

Trade became brisker than at Cook Strait—partly because Auckland had stronger links with Sydney, but also because its production was more diversified. It had kauri in the north, and later the gumfields. The Maoris, more numerous at Waitemata, were learning the use of money, and from the beginning were good spenders. They sold their produce in open market, going up the Waitemata in canoes laden with food; their labour was offered for wages; and for a time, until the pressure became too strong, they sold some at least of their tribal lands. Expansion was not easy, but it had an amplitude, a wide-ranging variety, which began to seem durable elements in the character of town and district.

There were setbacks and irritations, and the irritations were sometimes harder to bear than adversity. Queen Street was to grow into a thoroughfare so imposing that Aucklanders of later generations were not affronted when their city was described as the largest one-street town in the country. In the early days, however, the main shopping street became a quagmire in wet weather. Drainage was attempted by digging ditches so deep that pedestrians had to be protected from them by barricades; and in bad areas, particularly at the corner of Queen and Fort Streets, they seemed in appearance to anticipate trenches of the Western Front in the Great War of 1914-18.

The sudden rainstorms also flooded low-lying buildings. One of them was the Courthouse, which had been built in Queen Street when manuka was still growing nearby. Newspapers had long agitated for a building more in keeping with the needs and dignity of justice; and in 1863, when the courthouse and jail were again partly submerged, a newspaper recently founded, the *New Zealand Herald* (second of the name), opened fire in the emphatic style of colonial journalism: "Against the pollutions and miasmatic influences of this odious structure," the paper declared, "Chief Justice, grand jury and the voice of public opinion have been uplifted year after year in vain. Under its pestilential roof the Court undergoes some of the sufferings of the Black Hole of Calcutta. When is this filthy and feculent hovel, a disgrace to the finest street of the finest city of New Zealand, likely to be removed?"

Relief was not far away: the foundations of a Supreme Court were laid—on high ground—in 1865. The event was reported and celebrated in the columns of the *Herald*, but by that time the editorial guns had found a more substantial target. For 1865 was also the year in which Auckland ceased to be the capital of New Zealand.

The decision to move Parliament to Wellington was received around Cook Strait with enthusiasm. It was something, the old-timers said, that should have happened long ago. Men were still alive who remembered the frustration and disappointment of 1840; and at last the Wakefield enterprise was fulfilled and justified, though in circumstances rather different from those visualised by the founding fathers.

Auckland now felt the dismay and anger which had oppressed the early settlers at Port Nicholson. It was perhaps a little harder to accept the decision in 1865, since the town had had Government House (fully operative), and then Parliament, for a total of 25 years.

Ahirirangi, Mohaka (A. J. Cooper)
Well-watered valleys allowed Hawke's Bay to become one of the more
productive parts of New Zealand. Already, in 1861, green pasture and cultivated
land could be seen on the banks of the Mohaka River.

New Plymouth (Lt-Col. Chas E. Gold)
New Plymouth long remained an outpost; and in the 1860s, as the threat and
then the facts of war came to Taranaki, it became an armed camp, the small
town full of redcoats and simmering with warlike preparation.

The loss of Parliament meant a loss of prestige and power. More
significantly, it meant the loss of public servants and officials, and
therefore of business. Auckland had long shown a tendency to
separate itself (in thought and attitude, if not physically) from the
rest of New Zealand, and its awareness of identity, as a self-
contained community, was revealed now in editorial comment.

The *New Zealand Herald* carried anger to the verge of
incoherence. Southern provinces, the paper said, had banded
together "to oppress and cast down a powerful rival". It continued:
"The real object of the South in clinging so tenaciously to one
government for New Zealand is obvious enough. The Middle
Island provinces, with the exception of Nelson, are bankrupt, but
by political combination, and by buying Wellington support at the
price of the seat of government, they hope to keep the reins in the
hands of Southern men, and bolster up their failing credit by
association with the respectable, solvent names of Auckland and
Napier.

"Were New Zealand an independency our remedy would be
simple enough—an appeal to the arbitrament of the sword. As it
is, our appeal lies in the supreme power against the intolerance
which has wrested from us that share of representative government
accorded equally to the several provinces. This is the one great
cause of our desire for separation."

Significantly, it was the rest of the country (south of Napier),
and not merely Wellington, which had now become the Enemy.

114

Nelson (after Barraud)
By the time this picture appeared, in 1877, Nelson had triumphed over isolation and was growing into one of the colony's most attractive towns. A balance between nature and settlement, never too sharply disturbed by industry, had been preserved by people who loved trees and green places.

Talk of separation, and of "the sword", was mainly rhetoric; and in the next few years Auckland had other and more serious preoccupations. The war in Taranaki, which seemed to have ended in 1861, flared up again in 1863, and spread to the Waikato; and in 1865, when Parliament moved to Wellington, campaigns still had to be fought, and there would be news of outrage and exploit— including the hanging of the Rev C. S. Volkner at his church door in Opotiki, the massacre of 70 people at Matawhero, near Gisborne, and the long pursuit of the escaped "rebel", Te Kooti.

The war came close to Auckland, with skirmishes in outlying villages; and the young city must have been in a state of continuous preparation as gunboats went up the Waikato River, and news came in of victories and losses in districts not very far from Queen Street. Nevertheless, life went on without violent interruption inside a circle of blockhouses and under the protection of British regiments. The war ebbed into skirmish and sporadic outbreak, and ended at last when the elusive Te Kooti escaped to the King Country. Life became more secure, and the confiscation of Maori land opened new prospects for development—at a price in race relations which would not seem unduly high until the bill was presented again to later generations.

Meanwhile the 19th century was moving on through a flurry of progress, stimulated by one of the most inventive periods in history as scientists found new ways of harnessing natural energy. In 1865, while men with political leanings were still talking about the loss of Parliament, a diversion was caused by the first use of gas. People went out into the streets to observe the phenomenon: the *Herald* reported that Queen Street was "thronged until an advanced hour of the evening with moving crowds of gazers, who seemed never to weary of staring at the unwonted spectacle presented to them, while there were occasional 'rushes' into some of the other streets as the report spread of some particularly effective illumination". In those days, and long afterwards, people used the streets freely at night, unafraid of violence.

The wars had delayed road-making and the building of railways; but communications now began to improve, though not at first in any spectacular way. Travellers had had to ride horseback to the Waikato; but in 1870 they were able to go by coach, and the journey from Auckland to Hamilton, and back, took only two days. Far more exciting, about the same time, was a form of travel which appeared to be invisible. Editors of the *Otago Daily Times* and the *New Zealand Herald* exchanged telegrams of congratulations as Auckland attained "wire communication" with the rest of New Zealand.

The whole country was now moving forward, in social as well as physical exploration. Education became free and compulsory; a telephone was used for the first time in Christchurch; omnibuses were replaced by trams (pulled by horses, and then driven by steam and electricity); a phonograph was heard in Auckland, playing—to a bemused audience—a polka for cornet by "the lady champion of New York"; and, more wonderful still, the "first lady mayor in the British Empire", Mrs Elizabeth Yates, was installed as Mayor of Onehunga. And finally, at the end of the century, came the motor car. The *New Zealand Herald*, whose columns have supplied news items already quoted, welcomed it on a sour note: "As Auckland is by far the worst roaded place in New Zealand it is not likely that the fastest kind of motor car will become common, except in favoured districts, but it will not require a very fast motor car to compete against Auckland railways. . . ."

Wellington shared these gifts from the age of science; but its inhabitants often saw them differently, since social change had to be permitted by legislation, and even a new invention might require statutory treatment. The town continued to prosper, especially after the Wairarapa and the Manawatu were opened for farming; but its people were close to the big debates, and the emphasis began to move from trade to other preoccupations.

Hindsight may sometimes tempt us to believe that Wellington's destiny had seemed from the beginning to be political. It would be fanciful to suggest that the capital had been designed for its task by nature and history. Nevertheless the effects of situation and climate were reinforced by conditions of settlement, and above all by the imprint of the New Zealand Company.

The founding of Wellington was the Company's major venture, and it felt the considerable driving power of the Wakefields. Their supreme theorist, Edward Gibbon Wakefield, was to stay outside New Zealand until 1853; but he worked strenuously for Wellington,

Environs of Auckland (Alfred Sharpe) (Detail only)
Auckland was spreading in the 1870s, but gently, and without signs of haste.
People with stables, or within reach of horse-drawn omnibuses, could live
spaciously, untroubled by sounds of traffic or the radio next door.

View of Auckland Harbour (J. B. C. Hoyte)
In the later years of the 19th century Sir Frederick Whitaker, one of Auckland's most influential politicians and a Premier of New Zealand, could step from his house into this garden and look down on the city he had helped to guide through mid-century difficulties.

and more effectively than he was able to when he was at last on the scene, dabbling in politics. But the family was always there.

It was Colonel William Wakefield who organised the land-buying expedition of 1839, and became the settlement's leader. He was accompanied by Edward Jerningham Wakefield, his nephew; and Arthur Wakefield, brother of Edward Gibbon and William, was the Company's agent at Nelson until he was killed at Wairau. Daniel Wakefield, another of the brothers, came first to New Plymouth, but soon moved to the capital. The youngest brother, Felix, became a colonist in Canterbury.

There appears to have been no concerted planning by the Wakefields, and some members of the family were stronger and more talented than others. William and Arthur were outstanding as on-the-spot administrators and men of action; Daniel was undistinguished; and Edward Gibbon, subtle and complex, was eager for power and yet a man with a dream. He remained an intellectual, following his ideas by winding paths, and in the end falling short of rounded achievement, and reaching pathos instead of fame in his last days in Wellington. But the Wakefields were a formidable clan; and Wellington, in its formative years, was never without them. Other men might think of trade; the Wakefields could not walk down the street without being political.

Their influence remained after they were dead; but it was waning, and its real work had been done in the infant settlement.

118

One Tree Hill (W. Eastwood)
At the end of the 19th century the country around Auckland was pastoral, with farms at Panmure and One Tree Hill. The landscape had become partly European, protected by exotic trees, live hedges and stone walls. There was nothing, except an occasional motor car, to give warning of suburbs advancing.

In 1840 the immigrants at Petone were setting up the country's first organised colony, and they had been indoctrinated for the purpose. Many of them were "organisation" men, not in the narrow meaning of the word in later times, but in a sense strong enough to leave with them a need of union and debate and collective leadership. Men among them with capital and influence had attended meetings and joined a society of "intending colonists"; there had been pamphlets to read, speeches to hear; and labourers had assimilated ideas which began to have meaning when joined in memory to their experience of harsh conditions in England.

It was here, if anywhere, that politics entered the country ready-made. And with it came an adherence to the principles of British justice, an almost instinctive acceptance of "law and order". Government came down to Wellington as if to its true home; and thereafter, as a public service grew from small beginnings, the character of the place was determined irrevocably.

Government never ceases to fascinate men who love power; but it can be a distraction to ordinary people (and sometimes a form of licensed interference), and it can have strange and even paralysing effects on cities which are concerned too much with the business of Parliament. It may even be said that the least interesting cities in the world are those which have been built specially to house and serve politicians and public servants.

Wellington had its own life before it became the seat of government; and its harbour, beautiful and untameable, and its narrow streets, would preserve something untouchable and unique in its character as a town. But a certain restraint came to be felt, like an emanation from constricting hills, when Parliament Buildings appeared at last above Lambton Quay.

Auckland resented the loss of Parliament; and in 1865, when Parliament was still young, and the Public Service was rudimentary, its citizens could scarcely have suspected that the loss would free them for expansion. It was not easy afterwards to accept from Wellington a direction that was seen often as interference. Aucklanders wanted to make their own city and province. Regulations framed in a government department, and laws passed in the capital, had to be lived with, though not always gracefully; but there remained wide areas of independence, and these became wider still as population moved northwards.

Meanwhile Wellington was learning that the presence of Parliament was a doubtful blessing. In Auckland and Christchurch the civic leaders were tied by Acts of Parliament, but could still preside over little empires. The mayors and councils of Wellington were overshadowed by prime ministers and cabinets. They were always a step or two behind or below the politicians in precedence and occasion; and as the city tried to grow, and at last broke through to suburbs beyond the hills, it began to lose revenue. Land taken for government buildings was not rateable. At first, when these buildings were few and scattered, it did not matter; but it began to matter a great deal as the Public Service mushroomed in the 20th century.

New Plymouth and Nelson were also Company settlements. But they were smaller than Wellington, and were planned under different conditions. The northern settlement, organised at first by the Plymouth Company, was taken over by the larger company after settlers had arrived. These people came mainly from Devon and Cornwall, and appear to have met their early frustrations with with fortitude and good humour. They were isolated and short of land, and in the 1860s they suffered further delay and restriction when their town became an armed camp.

Nelson had similar problems. There were no serious clashes with the Maoris after the Wairau Affray; but the wars in Taranaki touched them, in some ways directly, as "refugees" arrived for billeting. The town and province remained isolated, and therefore a little outside the main political stream, though it produced some notable politicians, especially William Fox and David Monro. There are advantages in isolation, provided it is not absolute: the distant view is sometimes clearer than a close-up, and men who retire from the arena can return to it refreshed.

The arena itself has no respite. Wellington was not governing the country; it was merely the place from which the country was governed, and this meant a large element of transiency in the population. There were of course true Wellingtonians, devoted to their birthplace, and supported by people who succumbed to its special magic and became Wellingtonians by adoption. But the large infusion of outside blood, in an expanding public service,

Brougham Street (C. Aubrey)
Wellington was growing uncertainly in the 1890s. Big houses stood on hillsides near Mount Victoria, and would have decades of gentility before they were converted into flats and "bed-sitters"; but narrow streets were never far away. Everyone, however, was close to open spaces, and those who walked could walk safely.

and the growth of satellite towns where civil servants in large numbers built their homes, deprived the population of an earlier homogeneity.

The flavour of colonial life did not disappear quickly. In 1888, when a third child was born to Harold and Annie Beauchamp of Tinakori Road, Wellington was still a town with ample space and a character recognisably its own. The classless society had not yet arrived, though money rather than birth or station determined the lines of division. If segregation existed, it had an economic basis: the town sprawled uncertainly, as if neither the rich nor poor completely owned it. Narrow and congested streets would become slums, as Kathleen Beauchamp was to show later when she wrote "The Garden Party"; but the big houses were never far away, standing in large grounds above streets which carried vehicles drawn sedately by horses.

The place had a settled look, deceptively tranquil as we turn back to it today. Years later, when Kathleen Beauchamp was a restless adolescent, she complained of bareness, and could not accept colonial life. But people born under those ravaged hills and within sight of the harbour could not leave them in spirit, no matter how far they travelled from the streets of weatherboard houses. Kathleen became Katherine Mansfield, and seemed to find her true home in London; but in the end it was Wellington, remembered in love and anguish, which made her best known to the world.

Rivalry between Auckland and Wellington became less intense towards the end of the 19th century. Wellington had government; but Auckland could grow outwards, unimpeded, to the waters of two harbours and a rich countryside. It had population and wealth, and accepted with complacency a conviction—stated freely by civic leaders—that it would become a metropolis.

The feud of an earlier time came gradually to be seen as a joke, kept alive by newspaper columnists and speakers at luncheons. Sometimes, as Auckland showed again a disconcerting tendency to secede in spirit from the rest of the country, the witticisms may have taken an edge, and old tensions appeared still to be latent. But time and change were not to be stayed; and physical apartness, a first cause of distrust and rivalry, was soon to be overcome by fast travel and communication.

A traveller who sees today where Hamilton stands, with the environs of Auckland reaching down from the north, and its own suburbs and satellite villages extending almost solidly to Te Kuiti, may ask what rivalries of the past could survive this transformation as slowly, inexorably, the countryside is swallowed. But that will be a story for a century still to come.

The Pilgrim South.

In the later years of the 19th century a small man, barely 1.5 metres high, was seen around the streets of Dunedin, and was everywhere greeted with the respect usually reserved for men of larger stature. This was Thomas Hocken, doctor of medicine, and known widely outside his profession. Like many small men, he had abundant vitality. His photograph preserves a strong face, with the quizzical eyes of a man who has attended many bedsides and heard much of human folly and complaint. They are also tired eyes, narrowed a little above pouches, and showing the strain of long efforts to decipher poor and faded handwriting on documents grown yellow with age.

In the midst of his busy practice, and (for 22 years) as Dunedin's Coroner, Hocken found time to follow a consuming interest, the study of New Zealand history. He began with the settlement of Otago, but moved gradually to the whole field of ethnology in the Pacific basin. He also travelled extensively, in search of information, or as a pilgrim to scenes of historic events, especially places associated with the life and work of Samuel Marsden, a man he admired and venerated. It was Hocken who (in 1903) found Marsden's letters and journals at the offices of the Church Missionary Society in London. He brought them back in triumph, hoping to edit them for publication. This work had to pass into other hands; but without Hocken's efforts there would have been large gaps in New Zealand literature.

Dunedin 1849 (E. I. Abbott)
Dunedin was a year old when this settler and his family, obviously dressed for kirk, looked northwards to the town in 1849. They were living in Little Paisley, a district inhabited by weavers from that other Paisley, in Scotland, where unemployment had persuaded many workers to seek a new life overseas.

In 1897 he announced at a public meeting that his collection of historical records would be given to the city of Dunedin, if it could be "suitably housed". Thirteen years later, after money had been collected, and the usual negotiations had ended tardily in action, a new building was opened as a wing of the Otago Museum, and the priceless collection was in the care of the Council of the University of Otago. Hocken was too ill to attend the opening ceremony; he died a few weeks later.

The lives of collectors are not as a rule very rich in biographical interest. Alexander Turnbull, for instance, has become almost a shade, especially now that his books are no longer in the old brick building at the corner of Bowen Street. Bibliophiles are inclined to lose themselves in books, putting aside their own identities; and although their searches may be conducted skilfully and with great persistence, as if they were exercises in detection, they are overshadowed by the objects they pursued. They live vicariously, a paper existence, and are the moles of society, burrowing for treasure. We would all be poorer without them, but they are not easily recognisable as individuals when they emerge from libraries and come blinking into daylight.

Port Chalmers about 1849 (William Fox)
At Koputai, known later as Port Chalmers, Maori leaders assembled in 1844 to sign a deed which allowed their land to be bought for the Otago Block. Five years later the houses of new settlers stood between forest and waterfront.

Thomas Hocken was an exception. He was a doctor first, and a writer as well as a collector; and on at least one occasion the three personae came together, revealing a man behind them. The story is told in *Contributions to the Early History of New Zealand* (1898), a useful and entertaining guide for those who study the beginnings of Otago. It is also a book rich in anecdote, allowing history to take the flesh of people and move out from documents into the streets of Dunedin.

An old man was often seen in those streets, always alone, and always with a bundle tied to his back. Hocken was called to him as a doctor, and found him dying. Although he appeared to be poor, his landlady described him as a wealthy man. Hocken found that no will had been made, and proposed to make one on the spot for the old man's signature. But the would-be testator could think of no one close to him. At last, time running out, he remembered a wild night on the banks of the Clutha, and a runholder who took him into his home, saving him from cold and hunger.

"In this gentleman's favour," wrote Hocken, "the will was accordingly made." The doctor had done his duty, and the collector could now step forward. As "his part of the booty", he took charge of the mysterious bundle, "which contained some old and tattered New Zealand Company's Reports and other similar documents relating to the old man's claim to land".

Hocken belongs very much to the story of the South Island. Some of it he reported himself, always faithfully; and few who followed him have not been in his debt for painstaking research and a treasure of detail, exact and often curious. He may be seen as one of the island's symbolic figures, illustrating a true hunger of mind and spirit.

It can be claimed for Otago and Canterbury that settlement arrived with a sense of purpose not confined to material welfare. There was a lively interest in politics, especially when Wellington was leading the movement towards self-government; but the southern colonies were planned with a concern for religion and education: churches and schools were to be endowed from a proportion of the money paid for land. Although Hocken was an Englishman, arriving early enough (in 1862) to be an alien among the Scots, the spirit of inquiry that was so much a part of his life, the immense dedication and the sense of history, were attributes which from the first were respected in Otago and Canterbury.

There was, perhaps, more time to think of books and schools in these later provinces: the larger intellectual life of the south was in part a gift from the north, where men and women had learnt the hard way, with little guidance, what it meant to step ashore and start with bare hands to build a colony. Auckland had grown as if spontaneously, with the untidiness which is often a result of undirected vitality. Wellington was planned; but the plans were made without official approval or blessing, and were carried through at risk, with a boldness that—in the circumstances—was almost rashness. Otago and Canterbury were organised in co-operation with the New Zealand Company, but outside its control, and there had been time for lessons to be learnt from the Company's experience, and especially its mistakes. These were to

Dunedin 1862 (R. S. Kelly)
This watercolour of Dunedin was painted about a year after the discovery of gold, when the town had not yet received the full shock of invasion. It preserves a moment of pause, the colonial period ending, and the robust years of expansion about to begin.

be model settlements, organised carefully, and founded with strict legality.

Nevertheless, colonists could not escape the early shock, the reaction from euphoria. They felt the impact of strange hills, heavy with forest where they leaned at Dunedin towards the water, and bare and brown in the arrested lava-flow at Port Cooper. For them, too, was the unpacking, the building of huts, the cooking in sheds, with pots simmering weakly on fires that had to be guarded from rain, and outside their huts a muddy track, soon lost in an immense and brooding silence. It was the same primitive experience that men and women had known in the north: the struggle for a foothold, the effort to make a home for the family, and to take food from uncleared land.

At such times the finer side of life could scarcely go beyond a poem by Robert Burns, recited from memory; or a Bible read by candlelight, against the sound of a flute, melancholy in the distance; or a copy of the *Otago News*, passed from hand to hand once a fortnight because it cost sixpence and had to be cherished, in spite of writing and printing so poor that its motto—"There's pippins and cheese to come"—had a suggestion of mockery.

Further north, a year or two later, entertainment would be broader. Mr FitzGerald would bring together in Lyttelton some members of his glee club who had sung so sweetly on the *Charlotte Jane*, soothing passengers with concerts in the cuddy; and presently Mrs Godley, wife of the Canterbury Association's agent, would give a ball in the largest house in the town, not far from the immigration barracks, and equally exposed to the dust which blew in upon the dancers with a raging nor'wester. The inhabitants of both settlements had to make the best of things, and were generally able to do so. They were supported by hope and faith; and beneath their faith, at various depths, were influences from religion and the fellowship of a church.

The religious theme which shaped the first chapter of European occupation, in the Bay of Islands, reappeared in the colonisation of the south, but in a different form. Instead of a few missionaries, trying to introduce the Maoris simultaneously to civilisation and Christianity, members of the Church itself were now arriving. They were not a single body, united in spirit and practice: factions divided them, and conflicting opinions on doctrine and ritual. Nevertheless, they were professing Christians who were expected to be God-fearing people with virtues that would help to make New Zealand an ornament among the nations. Captain Cargill reminded his people of this when he welcomed them ashore from the *Philip Laing*: "The eyes of the British Empire, and I may say of Europe and America, are upon us. The work we do here will be observed, my friends, and it is our duty to do it worthily."

The colonisation of Otago and Canterbury had been planned for several years, among difficulties which provided a training ground for leadership. Only men of more than usual stamina and ability could have survived those testing years. Not surprisingly, therefore, the founding fathers had strong profiles. In Otago they also had a Scottish dourness.

Christchurch 1850 (Fitch)
Edward Ward, a passenger from the *Charlotte Jane*, inspected the site of
Christchurch. "Here," he wrote, "beside a clear-flowing river, a solitary house
full of baggage . . . and unoccupied, a stack of sawn timber and one boat, there
was no sign of town or city." This scene was painted a few months later.

Unlike the young men who led the Canterbury Pilgrims,
William Cargill and the Reverend Thomas Burns were almost
patriarchal. Burns was 47 when he was one of 400 ministers who
left the Established Kirk of Scotland in 1843 to set up the Free
Church, rebelling against patronage and an oppressive spiritual
direction; and he was 52 when he landed from the *Philip Laing*.
Captain William Cargill was older still at 64, a veteran of the
Peninsula Campaign and a disciplinarian, contriving by sheer
strength of character to overcome the disadvantages of small stature
and a slightly comic appearance.

The man who first devised the Otago scheme, George Rennie,
could not stand against Burns and Cargill in the lobbying which
preceded the formation of a controlling body, the Lay Association
of the Free Church. Rennie was an intellectual, and may have
been influenced by Edward Gibbon Wakefield, who was never far
away when new colonies were being planned. His ideas, as
expounded in the *Colonial Gazette* of London, appear in retrospect
to have been simple enough; but they promised order instead of
improvisation. First, he argued, a site should be selected and
surveyed. Engineers would lay out the town and build a wharf;
land would be cleared, sown in crops, and stocked with cattle.
Not until then would the first colonists be sent out from Scotland.
Suburban and rural sections would be waiting, and the colony
would begin at once to be self-supporting.

Mosgiel (unknown)
Mosgiel still had a rural look in 1885, but it was already known for its woollen mill, and was sharing the industrial activity which made Dunedin prosperous after new wealth came in from the goldfields.

Events did not work out as Rennie had planned, and he was nudged from the leadership by Cargill and Burns, who had now identified themselves closely with the scheme. Rennie had seen the Free Church movement as a useful lever for emigration, but he was a broad-minded man who wanted to avoid sectarianism. Burns and Cargill insisted that ministers and teachers were to come from the Free Church, and that this church alone should receive endowments. By then, however, agreement had been reached between the New Zealand Company and the Lay Association on terms of purchase, and the movement began to gain momentum.

The British Government had to be pushed towards approval, and at no time showed enthusiasm for settlement of the Middle Island. Its attitude may have had more to do with inertia than with policy. Few difficulties were expected from Maoris: they were not numerous enough to be troublesome over land-titles, although they did cause some delays, especially near Akaroa. In the 1840s, however, not more than 500 Maoris were living between the Hurunui and Waitaki Rivers; and in 1844, when Frederick Tuckett had completed his survey of 161,874 hectares for the Otago Block, only about 150 natives—men, women and children—assembled at Port Chalmers to witness the signing of a deed which alienated their land forever for the sum of £2,400.

Reluctance to occupy the island may have had its source in dispatches from Auckland. Governors had found it difficult enough

Reid's Flourmill (C. Aubrey)

Southland in the 1880s was recovering from its ill-timed separation from Otago, and was overcoming the difficulties of isolation and small markets. This flourmill at Gummies' Bush was one of many enterprises which helped to support small but independent communities.

to govern the North Island and Nelson settlements without having to extend their authority and narrow resources to broad lands in the south. They had learnt that colonists became stiff-necked and independent in their isolated towns, and talked too soon of self-government. In the end, however, the New Zealand Company was allowed to buy land and re-sell it, under certain conditions, to the lay body of the Free Church, and later to the Canterbury Association, a group as enthusiastic as the Scots for church settlement, but seeing it in broader terms.

By the late 1840s it must have been obvious, even to unresponsive bureaucrats at the Colonial Office, that the South Island would colonise itself if Government declined to act. The movement had started before Rennie produced his scheme. As early as 1840 a few families from New South Wales landed at Port Cooper and began to farm at Putaringamotu, on the edge of the Riccarton bush. These people stayed 18 months, and abandoned their farms when titles to the land came into question; but the Deans brothers arrived in 1843, and at that time the property of Captain W. B. Rhodes on Banks Peninsula—the first cattle station in the South Island—had been occupied for several years. The French had reached Akaroa in 1840; and further south, along the east coast, were whaling stations which became the nuclei of agricultural settlements. There was even, at Waikouaiti, a Wesleyan mission house.

John Jones, a whaler with large ideas, brought some families from Sydney to his station at Waikouaiti; and by 1848, when the first immigrants reached Otago, his farms were large enough to supply the new settlement with meat and vegetables. A few people had drifted down from Wellington and Nelson; and these families, several runaway sailors, and an advance party of surveyors, were living in bays around Dunedin when Captain Cargill and Mr Burns brought their flock to anchorage.

Cargill had a position of undisputed authority, and held it for the rest of his life. He was appointed Resident Agent for the New Zealand Company; a few years later, when the Company was no longer operating, and the Lay Association disbanded, he became Commissioner of Crown Lands. The Rev. Thomas Burns was described officially as the Minister to accompany the first party of settlers; but although the Church was his abiding concern, he was influential in public affairs, at all times ready to act as the conscience of the little community when it showed signs of disregarding Christian principles.

These two were an interesting pair: Cargill with his short body and large head, his enormous bonnet and rapid step; and Burns, tall and dignified, slower of speech but slow also to stop when speech had begun, and paternal in a Victorian way, with a vein of sternness through his benevolence. They were different in appearance and method, yet somehow complementary. In long diplomacy, when emigration was being planned, they had found they could work together, and they continued in the settlement to operate a joint leadership, tacit rather than formal, but accepted almost without question.

Their task was by no means easy. The Godleys spent Easter in Cargill's home in 1850, on their way to Lyttelton; and already, less than two years after the founding of Dunedin, the visitors could see evidence of discord. "There is a Scotch and an English party," wrote Charlotte Godley in *Letters from Early New Zealand* (1951), "and half of them will not visit the other half, or approve of anything that is done." She added, with characteristic good sense: "I believe it is so more or less in all small communities, and here *Scotch* and *English* of course makes a capital ground of offence." She returned to the subject a little later, summing up her impressions: "Altogether it is much what I expected to find, except that I thought, in a colony, people would have been more friendly and fond of each other and less upon form. There is as much etiquette about visiting, and so on, at Dunedin as I ever saw anywhere at home. . . ."

The Scottish character has always had a special interest for the English; but even Dr Johnson, in spite of his more outrageous criticism, was attracted as well as repelled: he could not otherwise have endured so much of his gossip-in-waiting, Jamie Boswell. In Otago, a long way from home, the Scots continued to be themselves, resisting transplantation, and preserving their dialect. Although Burns and Cargill had tried to organise an emigration confined to members of the Free Kirk, they had not succeeded; some of the colonists, indeed, were not even Presbyterian. To a certain extent, however, the presence of strangers may have been a necessary

Invercargill (R. P. MacGoun)
Invercargill was a town of the plains, and its planners used ample space. The wide streets may have seemed a little bare in 1886, when this watercolour was painted; but they accepted without strain the traffic and taller buildings of a later time.

irritant, helping Presbyterians to be more truly themselves while they closed their ranks against heretics and outsiders.

Under these conditions there soon emerged what Hocken—mildest of critics—could only describe as "the unfortunate habit of bickering". It may have been nothing more than a Scottish need to question, to argue, and to oppose. Without a leavening of the English, progress might have been slower, since it is harder to get things done when everybody has different and equally firm views on policy. The cast of mind we know best through Carlyle was always present in Dunedin. It is doubtful if a preference for dogma, and the use of monologue instead of conversation, produce the most successful politicians; but they indicate strong feeling and opinion that create a climate which politicians find congenial.

There was no shortage of grievances, soundly based. The settlers were frequently in agitation as rumours of new iniquity reached them. Some questions were being debated throughout New Zealand: for example, Earl Grey's proposal that convicts should be sent out from England after they had served the main part of their sentence at home. The promise of cheap labour could not prevail against a strong aversion to the transportation system, and perhaps it was too soon for the needs of convicts themselves, and especially their need of rehabilitation, to receive serious attention.

FIRST POST OFFICE Ch: Ch:
1857

Mesopotamia (Wm Packe)
Samuel Butler came to Canterbury in 1860 and stayed only four years; but he wrote an excellent report on the settlement, explored headwaters of the Rakaia and Rangitata, and influenced the intellectual life of Christchurch with articles in early issues of the *Press*. This is where he lived, at "Mesopotamia".

First Post Office, Christchurch (Geo. Turner)
Canterbury's first post office was at Lyttelton, close to the incoming ships. In 1858, a full-time postmaster was appointed in Christchurch, looking after mails in the building shown at the left of this picture.

Gloucester Street, Christchurch, 1857 (Emily Harper)
Bishop Harper's daughter painted Gloucester Street in 1857. The hills are
closer than they seem to be today, and the stream is narrower; but the houses
have the true character of their time, substantial, and built to last. They are
standing on ground near the present centre of Christchurch.

As elsewhere in New Zealand, land was always the subject of
complaint and debate. There was no Maori problem; but the
New Zealand Company, responsible for surveys and emigration,
had not opened up enough country outside the town; and the Lay
Association, which had undertaken to sell 2,000 properties in five
years, had to admit in 1851 (when it was no longer tied to the
Company) that so far it had failed. The colony was badly in need
of roads and more capital.

Little assistance, and less sympathy, could be expected from the
Government. Sir George Grey, especially, was unsympathetic. He
was, said Hocken, "a determined opponent of the class settlements
of Otago as well as Canterbury, because, it was said, they were
independent of his autocratic rule". Grey was not without support
in Dunedin: the English settlers were said to think as he did.
Although they may not have wanted a continuance of "autocratic
rule", they shared Grey's distrust of settlement based on religious
doctrine. It was now, as political and religious prejudice collided,
that the English of Otago became the "Little Enemy". New land
regulations were to bring improvements in 1855, and by then the
Governor's long shadow was receding. The Constitution Act of
1852 had come into effect, and New Zealanders were at last to have
self-government.

Upper Harbour, Dunedin (John Gibb)
Dunedin was an industrial city in 1887, and cargoes were passing through in growing volume. This picture of the Upper Harbour shows sail and steam together; but steam was gradually prevailing.

News that the Bill had been passed reached Dunedin in November 1852. It was received with excitement and rejoicing which can scarcely have been equalled elsewhere in the country. People ran through the muddy streets as the town crier made his announcement; a gun at the jetty was fired, after several attempts; a little bell rang continuously; and tar-barrels were set alight and thrown into the harbour. In spite of rain, there was dancing on the jetty, and "tallow dips" appeared in every window, a form of illumination which in those days was pious rather than spectacular. The worst of their troubles, the citizens believed, were over.

If the Promised Land was at last in sight, only one man could be expected to lead them on the rest of the journey. Next day a deputation waited upon Captain Cargill, asking him to be a candidate for the office of Superintendent of the Provincial Council. During the colony's first five years the small person (and the large bonnet) of the Resident Agent had stayed immovably at the centre of dissension and disturbance. Undoubtedly he knew his people, showing the right amount of shrewdness in his dealings with them, and reserving intolerance for the Little Enemy. They had learned to trust him.

Cnr Hereford Street & Oxford Terrace (Geo. Turner)
In 1863 the corner of Hereford Street and Oxford Terrace was still near the edge of Christchurch. The streets were wide, and bridges were soon spanning the Avon; but pedestrians had to bend to the dust in summer and walk delicately through mud when the rains came.

The Constitution Act created six provinces. Otago was the lower third of the South Island, extending from the Waitaki River in the north to the coastline at Awarua Bay. To control this large area (much of it still unexplored), nine councillors and a superintendent, elected independently, would be committed to office by 264 electors, 78 in the town and 186 in the country. The council was empowered by the Act to pass ordinances that would have to be approved by the General Government in Auckland. In the meantime, however, this government did not exist.

Everybody in Dunedin was ready and eager for action; but there was procrastination, as always, in the north, and it was nearly a year before councils could be elected throughout New Zealand. This was a vexatious time, harder to bear after so much excitement; but at last, late in 1853, elections were held—openly, for all to see, in the manner of the period; and Captain Cargill duly became the first Superintendent.

Familiar names were on the list of councillors. W. H. Cutten, editor of the *Otago Witness*, and respected for his use of both pen and cudgel (he once manfully repulsed an attack on his person by a pack of Little Enemies) headed the town poll with 54 votes. The largest vote from country districts was given to John Harris, a lawyer. Behind him was James Macandrew, an enterprising merchant who had arrived in his own schooner to open a joint stock bank and to trade expansively. He had brought with him a quantity of bank-notes which turned out to be unusable under regulations of that time; but he was not the man to be dismayed by a setback, and was soon organising a currency of promissory notes, competing with Johnny Jones in attempts to corner the money market, and heading at a good round pace for a financial showdown and a taste of prison.

The first session of the Provincial Council opened on December 30, 1853 in the Mechanics' Institute. The surroundings were modest, even poor; but councillors and a few onlookers enriched them with a strong sense of occasion. Everything was arranged with strict formality, much as it would have been in the Mother of Parliaments. Hocken describes the scene in one of the best passages in his book: "A Speaker, in the person of Mr Macandrew, was elected, and he was then solemnly conducted to his chair. Then entered His Honour the Superintendent, all standing to receive him. The Rev. Thomas Burns acted as chaplain and said prayers. Following this the Superintendent delivered a lengthy inaugural address—equivalent to the Speech from the Throne; this concluded, he withdrew, all standing as before, and after some formal business the House adjourned."

If someone with a sense of humour had been the Superintendent, proceedings might have been more relaxed; but the times were serious, and councillors would have been unable to see themselves as actors in a charade. They were there by grace of a handful of electors (since only men could vote, and then only if they owned, leased or rented property of a specified value); but 2,000 people were in the Otago Block, and 2,400 in the province as a whole. A solid 700 were in the town of Dunedin: the rest were scattered abroad in pockets and outposts. A year's revenue for the

Camp on River Courtenay (Sir Fred. Weld)
Charlotte Godley wrote letters about life in Canterbury, not knowing that she
would keep the times alive for later generations. In 1850 she stood with her son
Arthur, looking across the Waimakariri towards Mount Grey. Camping, she
thought, was "the best fun possible, except at dressing-time".

council might be £3,000, and expenditure was about half as much.
But the place was growing. Sheep-runs were being taken up under
a licensing system for "depasturage", and 70,000 sheep were already
grazing throughout the province. Were these to be seen as laughing
matters?

The council that went solemnly about its business, in rented
premises, believed itself to be legislating for the future. Cargill
had reminded immigrants in 1848 that the eyes of Europe and
North America were upon them; and although it was unlikely that
London and New York would be aware of proceedings in Dunedin
five years later, it was prudent to behave as if they were and needed
to know that the proprieties had been observed in the true spirit
of democracy. And so the charade continued: "An executive was
formed, there was a ministerial crisis, a vote of want of confidence,
a resignation and a new-formed ministry. Messages were sent
down to the House, a gazette published, and one Proclamation at
least issued from 'Government House', meaning thereby, the pretty
cottage of the Superintendent."

Progress was not allowed to continue without interruption,
even when the General Assembly had at last been convened and
attempts were made to remove confusion over the possession of
land. Knowledge of the land itself, in Otago, was still imperfect.
Dunedin was at the edge of a region which stretched inland to

141

lakes and mountains known at first by rumour, and then from the tales of a few bold travellers. Southwards the margins grew misty in a country dismissed by Tuckett as unsuitable for farming, or even for habitation. This was Murihiku, home of a few Maoris who frequented the muttonbird islands below Rakiura. Its only European visitors, so far, had been sealers and whalers. The sealers had long since vanished, but a few whalers still touched the southern coasts.

A man named John Kelly, who had served on a whaler, went far enough inland to decide for himself that the country might after all be habitable. This was in 1853, about the time that the whole of Murihiku was bought from the Maoris, though not with any plans for early settlement. Kelly went up to Dunedin and married a Scottish widow. In 1855 he and his wife travelled by sea to Bluff, going afterwards up the Oreti. They were the first European settlers on land that was to become the site of Invercargill.

This was another of those spontaneous movements which occurred throughout the colonial story. For what reasons did Kelly and his wife go out to live in a tent or a hut in that solitary and rather forbidding place? What prospect of advancement, of future wealth or mere subsistence, could they have seen on the banks of the Oreti, with plains and forest moving back—under skies often grey and drizzling—to the Takitimu?

If they wanted good land, they had chosen wisely; but it seems unlikely that Kelly had money to lease and stock a farm. Instead he became a boatman, keeping to a trade he knew, and ferried new settlers up the river from Bluff. No doubt he was merely restless, used to a hard life and wanting to free himself from restraints already being felt in Dunedin. Every settlement had such people from the earliest times, responding in an instinctive way to an emptiness they saw as freedom. Always they moved further into the wilderness, pushing against an invisible frontier, and leaving a few faint traces—a track returning to bush, a little firewood, the slabs of a ruined hut—for those who came after.

The Kellys were not left long in solitude. Settlers came down, a few at a time, and in 1856 a small ship, the *Star*, brought 30 passengers to Bluff. A year later a post office was opened, and the first sections were sold on a town-site selected by John Thomson, the Otago surveyor. At this point a name was needed; and the Governor, Colonel Thomas Gore Browne, was at hand to supply one. At a banquet in Dunedin, wanting to pay a compliment to the Superintendent, he suggested that the new town in the south be named Invercargill. Even now, if we listen hard enough, we can hear the applause which greeted the proposal.

Browne liked to find names for places, and was better at it than most of his contemporaries. New Zealand suffered much in those times, and earlier, from men who had to fill blank spaces on maps. They were in a hurry to lay out a town, to identify streets, to attach labels to parcels of land and natural features; and unless they were unusually sensitive or imaginative, they turned with relief to the commonplace.

Attempts to avoid the commonplace were sometimes as unfortunate as eager acceptance. People who do not read poetry

Mornington Tramway (John Crawford)
The little trams of Mornington seem quaint today; but in 1885, as an old
gentleman sat deep in thought and a small girl watched the roadway demurely,
a cable car was Change itself, rattling at 24 kilometres an hour towards a future
full of surprises.

live today in streets named after poets; and the repetition of a few
names, when invention faltered, has caused postal confusion in
both islands. And what is to be said of a creek near Dunedin that
was named after a surveyor called Scroggs?

While such atrocities were being committed, alas, Maori names
were put aside by people unable to pronounce them, or
unresponsive to their music and rich associations. Yet it may be
unfair to forgotten worthies, including Mr Scroggs, to blame them
for not learning in a few months the lessons that are still being
spelt out for their descendants, generations later.

Invercargill had a population of 1,000 when the town received
a name. Four years later it became the capital of a separate
province. Otago had always felt itself to be neglected or badly
treated by the central government; and in the same way people
in its own outlying region believed that not enough money and
support were coming to them from the provincial capital. Similar
discontents were reported from other provinces; but inhabitants of
the far south passed from protest to action.

Separation was ill-timed. Two months after it was proclaimed
by Order-in-Council, Gabriel Read found gold in Otago, and the
new province of Southland was denied its share of the wealth that

143

soon began to flow into Dunedin. Even without this loss, the population would have been too small to provide resources needed for expansion, or indeed for survival; and in 1871, after 10 hard and debt-ridden years, the southern region again became part of Otago. Five years later the provincial governments were abolished. Thereafter provincial rivalry was vestigial, reserved mainly for football matches, as Wellington became the power-centre, and the universal target for complaint and criticism.

Northern Otago ended at the Waitaki River, and beyond it the colonists of Canterbury, rather loosely known as Pilgrims, were learning to live in their own way with the problems of settlement. They shared some of Dunedin's interests: the need to escape from restrictive notions of farming (imposed on them by the New Zealand Company) into the larger freedoms of pasture, and of course a firm opposition to the Auckland Government, the Governor and most officials. But some preoccupations were peculiarly their own, and these came from the land itself, the natural environment they were trying to see henceforth as home.

Elsewhere in New Zealand the colonists had entered forest, or had found it leaning towards their harbours and clearings. Canterbury was different, though equally forbidding to people sensitive to *genius loci*. Surveyors and farmers, looking closely at the land, might be able to see its richness; but immigrants, many without knowledge of farming, had to judge it from the outside. They saw first the bare hills of Lyttelton, enclosing a good harbour, but refusing them access to the plains. And when, climbing to summit or saddle, they could see the plains, they saw swamp and tussock, and more swamp, and empty land going back hazily to the mountains.

A few patches of forest survived, mere remnants of primeval growth—one at Riccarton, where the Deans brothers had shown what could be done with the land, and another about 30 kilometres northwards, in a place the Maoris called Rangiora. The rest of the plain was bare, or covered by tussock and matagouri, a sort of fuzz across the face of the earth.

Beneath the fuzz, however, the plain was richly alluvial. It had been built, in unimaginable reaches of time, on a bed of shingle brought down by rivers from the mountains. The soil was rich beyond a farmer's dreams, and virgin. But it had no protection from the prevailing north-west wind. This could become a great stream of air, drained of moisture in its passage across the Alps, and hot and searing as it moved towards the eastern coast. Colonials soon learnt about it, cowered from the dust which rolled before it when roads were built, and saw quickly the need for shelter.

Unlike their countrymen in Otago, and in most parts of the North Island, the Pilgrims did not have to make room for houses and farms by destroying forest. Instead, they set out to plant trees of their own. Plantations grew around homesteads; lines of willows appeared on the banks of rivers, especially the Avon; and orchards began to soften half-acre sections in the infant town of Christchurch.

Trees on the farmlands were mostly exotics, Californian radiata pine and some eucalypti from Australia; and in spite of the wind

Akaroa (Nicholas Chevalier)
Whalers were in Akaroa before the French came; but access from the plains
was difficult, and the place remained apart until the arrival of motor cars.
Isolation was long enough to preserve the town's unique character as a French
settlement on the shores of the "long harbour".

Lyttelton Harbour 1884 (T. Cane)
By 1884 the approaches to Lyttelton were much as travellers see them today:
narrow water between the moles, an inner harbour, and beyond it the roads
lifting to brown summits. Older houses were already becoming relics of colonial
times. But many ships still came in under canvas.

they gripped the soil with strong and spreading roots. Shelter belts became a new and increasingly familiar feature of the landscape. As the country became more settled, and the open runs were fenced, farmers experimented with live hedges, sometimes dangerously, as with gorse—yellow and beautiful in its flowering time, but insidious as it reached across the pasture.

Few landscapes can have been changed so thoroughly and in so short a time by creative methods. Mistakes were made until farmers began to understand the country. The primal growth of tussock, matagouri and speargrass was burnt in great fires, and burnt again—too often, and recklessly—as the matting reappeared; but trees were grown assiduously, and not merely for shelter. The settlers, after all, had come from parts of England where trees and hedgerows had belonged immemorially to the landscape.

Christchurch was part of the plain, with inhabitants whose business it was to provide goods and services for people coming and going (on horseback or in drays) across the farmlands; and here too the flatness was soon being relieved or softened by trees. A green smudge appeared on the banks of a river which followed a winding course to the estuary, and beyond it were stronger colours in orchards and gardens. For a long time the earth resisted, producing dust in summer and mud in winter; but the settlers used gardens, perhaps more than anywhere else in the country, to give their plain the appearance of home.

Beneath the effort may have been a subliminal need to identify and possess, not to be brought to the surface until there was time to stop and think, and even to write poetry. Ursula Bethell, who wrote long afterwards in a cottage on Cashmere Hills, may have caught the mood in a few lines from a poem called "Time":

'Established' is a good word, much used in garden books,
'The plant, when established' . . .
Oh, become established quickly, quickly, garden!
For I am fugitive, I am very fugitive—

The love of gardens and open spaces was expressed in a practical way when land was set aside for parks and reserves. It was done generously, and Christchurch appeared to be safe from encroachment as land became harder to find. Yet here, as elsewhere, the struggle had to be joined between those who wanted to preserve green places and those who saw land as a commodity with a market value, to be bought and sold for profit, and above all to be used.

In 1878, when the town was less than 30 years old, a politician suggested that 20 hectares along the northern and western borders of Hagley Park should be cut into building sections and leased to the public. The aim, ostensibly, was to find money to maintain and improve the rest of the park; but it was seen as an attempt to destroy the park, and was opposed with indignation. This was the first of many such attempts, leading always to controversy and resistance, and reaching their most dangerous point in the dinosaur-time of motorways.

The surprising fact is not the conflict itself, but its early appearance. True, the settlement and the province had to meet serious difficulties. Sheep-farmers were prosperous in the good

Timaru (Thos Babington)
This house in Timaru illustrates changes in the landscape as colonists
overcame the bareness of the plains, using exotic trees for shelter, and building
homes with a promise of gracious living. But only the few could afford them.

years, but the province as a whole was short of money. One of the
earliest needs was to bring Lyttelton Harbour closer to the plains.
It was done first by making a road, and then by a railway tunnel,
started before there was a railway, and completed at great cost but
triumphantly, in a pioneering achievement by engineers. The man
behind the scheme was William Sefton Moorhouse, the province's
second superintendent, and standing alongside John Godley and
James Edward FitzGerald among the founders and leaders of
Canterbury.

Godley was respected and acclaimed as the principal founder.
He was the Canterbury Association's agent; but he stayed less than
three years, and although in that time he worked hard for the
colonists, he was not a strong man physically, and a long tussle with
the Association's committee in London almost defeated him.
Godley was quick to see that the future of farming would be with
sheep rather than agriculture. In the end he made a radical
decision, and on his own initiative changed the regulations laid
down in London to prevent the leasing of pastoral lands. His
decision was endorsed five years later by the Provincial Council,
and was shown then to have been wisely taken.

Godley was a gentleman, a word used precisely in those days to
describe a man of gentle birth. He was also a Dubliner, a
Protestant, and deeply religious. In manner and in speech he was
correct and perhaps a little dry, and too fastidious to be at ease

with ordinary men. The colonists called him Old Jack, but more from colonial habit than from familiarity. His wife spoke of him in her letters with unquestioned loyalty, and echoed his opinions; and if no warmth of a personal relationship entered her pages it may have been because she was a Victorian wife, and reticent by nature and training.

Godley's close friend, James Edward FitzGerald, was in some ways his opposite, as friends often are. Although he was born in England, he too was from Anglo-Irish stock, and had received a stronger infusion of Irish blood, or at least of temperament. FitzGerald was versatile, and more of an artist than anything else. He liked to wear picturesque clothes; he loved to sing, especially in glee clubs; and he delighted in conversation. As the first editor of the *Lyttelton Times*, and for some years the editor and virtual proprietor of the *Press*, he had ample scope for his gifts as a writer. He tried to be a farmer, not very successfully, and did much better as a resident magistrate.

FitzGerald liked to speak and write as an architect. His ideas were definite, but he made no allowances for the rough edges of colonial life, the shortages of labour and material which forced builders to improvise. He condemned, for instance, the practice of imitating stone in timber—a practice which created the wooden section of the Provincial Chambers, valued later and preserved as a charming imitation of early Gothic. But many today would share his love of the gable, "the noblest form in architecture . . . running, where both faces are equal, into the pinnacle and spire".

A man who talked as freely as FitzGerald had to be a politician. He was, however, more at home in the Provincial Chambers than in the General Assembly, and he played no large part in national politics. Most of all, perhaps, he was a good writer and talker, without the narrower interests which allow some men to channel their energies towards a single and overriding purpose.

It was such a man, Henry Sewell, who came to Christchurch in 1852 to wind up the Canterbury Association's affairs, and thereafter to be busy, captious, and moderately successful in politics. He was, very briefly, the country's first Premier, and afterwards declined through shortish Cabinet appointments towards retirement. Sewell was capable, with ideas which may now seem often to have been correct; but he was sharply critical of men he could not understand, and tactless in dealing with them. Although he worked hard for Canterbury, especially while the Association's assets were being transferred to the province, his career in politics belonged to the wider scene, and he left no strong imprint, as a person, on the life of Christchurch.

Godley, FitzGerald and Moorhouse remain outstanding as men who stay alive for later generations. All three could be practical, although FitzGerald and Moorhouse (who were strong opponents, especially over the tunnel scheme) seemed to reserve practicality for public life, and were somewhat inadequate in their private affairs, a contradiction not unusual among politicians.

"Safe" men were never far away, headed by Samuel Bealey and William Rolleston, both sound administrators, though without a flair for leadership, the common touch or the hint of flamboyance

Christchurch about 1888
Most of the buildings in Cathedral Square in the late 1880s have long
disappeared, and those that remain are under threat of demolition. But the
city stays recognisable, its character emerging—even for those who do not
remember horse-drawn traffic—in the long flat streets, the low hills beyond,
and the tufted trees.

Christchurch Shops (Sidney Smith)
In 1884 these shops had long served the people of Christchurch (and service in
those days was individual, expert and patient); but now tall buildings, including
the handsome post office, were rising above them, and they were soon to be
replaced.

The Kaikoura Coast (John Gully)—transparency marked 209
Captain Cook named the Kaikouras the "Snowey Mountains", but an earlier
name for the whole region survived from Maori legend. Kaikoura has famous
fishing grounds, and became a holiday resort. For a long time, however, most
travellers saw it only from the sea, remembering a lovely coastline guarded by
mountains.

which allow plain men to see an enlargement of themselves in the men they like to follow.

Were the leaders founding the sort of community visualised by Wakefield and Godley when the Canterbury Association was formed in London? And what of the other church settlement, in Otago? Cargill and Burns were also pilgrims, more consciously so than the Canterbury leaders. Could it be said of their pilgrimage that the dream had been fulfilled?

There was really no dream apart from a wish to build communities that would be God-fearing and prosperous. In Dunedin the people were to be predominantly Scots, and members of the Free Church; Christchurch was to have Anglicans. The planners and founders believed that this exclusiveness was desirable, even necessary, if the colonies were to be successful; they were not wise enough to understand (as Sir George Grey probably did) that exclusiveness becomes narrowness, and stifles an expanding spirit.

Cargill, Burns and Godley were men of their times, and the times were unsettling for churchmen as religion came under scientific examination. It may have been tempting, in those days, to believe that the churches could put down their roots in a virgin soil, gaining new strength from it, and perhaps shielded from a chilling breeze of atheism that was beginning to blow across Europe.

In both provinces, however, exclusiveness was never absolute; and the great body of colonists, it may be supposed, were Sunday churchmen, reserving their energies for activities of a practical sort. They included pious men and women, and some bigots; and at times, when the Catholic Church began to make headway in the south, it seemed as if religious feeling had been stronger than an observer might have suspected. But sectarianism had little to do with true religion.

A riot in Christchurch on December 27 1879, when Orangemen marching to the station were attacked by a loitering mob with stones and pick-handles, was an example of enmity imported across the world from an unhappy past. On that day the police were below strength, and the Mayor hastily swore in 250 special constables to restore order. "But probably the most effective measure," said the *Christchurch Star*, reporting the event, "was the swift action of the Rev. Father Ginaty in braving the stones, flying fists and weapons to make an appeal to his people." The feelings on both sides were real enough, but the cause was already vestigial, and would be replaced soon enough by causes more openly political.

Religious loyalties, or adherence to any particular church, failed to have a strong or lasting effect on colonial life. It had seemed possible, however, that regional influences would be felt in the formation of a national character. Scots in Otago and Englishmen in Canterbury sometimes appeared to belong to separate cultures. They wore different clothes and spoke with different accents, almost in foreign tongues. If Scots dialects, or a suggestion of Gaelic, may still be heard in the far south, what could have happened to voices of the region if they had remained in long isolation?

There was isolation for a time, and it did more than preserve a dialect. Clannishness grew up in Otago and Southland; but so also did a communal warmth, self-reliance in local affairs, and a large hospitality. In recent times, before isolation was finally destroyed by air travel and broadcasting, the friendliness of people in Southland or Westland had become proverbial. Among them, too, were habits in speech and behaviour, and even physical characteristics, which at once identified a native inhabitant.

In the later colonial period, when self-government had at last been won, the provinces were like little states on their own, separated from one another by empty country. It was remarkable indeed that so much was done, under these conditions, to organise the beginnings of unity. News that the Constitution Act had been passed was brought to Port Chalmers by a schooner, the *Endeavour*, which needed a week for its voyage from Lyttelton. An overland journey from Dunedin to Christchurch took 12 days and was rarely attempted. And Dunedin's Members of Parliament were two months on their voyage to attend the first session of the General Assembly in Auckland.

If these conditions had continued for a century, instead of a few decades, the nation's character would have received a stronger imprint from the provinces. But regional differences became shallow as communications improved. In Otago, where a distinctive culture was most likely to evolve, the discovery of gold had a shattering effect. The sudden influx of people brought prosperity; but it was a large wave from the outside world that never entirely receded. Steam travel at sea, and the electric telegraph, continued the breakdown of isolation.

A nation's culture needs variety for enrichment. It seemed possible, as the 19th century neared its close, that this would have to be found somehow, somewhere, in the European population. The Maoris were depleted in number, dispirited by the loss of a large part of their tribal lands, and sinking into a second-class status. They were described frequently as a dying race.

The story of their recovery is outside the scope of this book. But enough may have been said here to illustrate the mingling of Maori and European themes in our colonial history. And history does not stop; it cannot be closed as a book is closed, but flows on in the blood of new generations, in feelings inherited, and in ideas shaped by what happened long ago in the Bay of Islands, outside the stockades of Taranaki, on the plains of Canterbury, and among the hills of Otago. The mingling of two races, not only physically, but by interfusion of cultures, in conflict as well as acceptance and understanding, now gives life in New Zealand its strongest creative impulse.

List of Illustrations

CHAPTER ONE

Page 8. "Waterfalls in the Otira Gorge", 1891 oil by Petrus van der Velden. *Dunedin Art Gallery*

Page 9. "Te Tarata White Terraces", 1877 lithograph after Charles Decimus Barraud. *Alexander Turnbull Library*

Pages 10-11. Mount Egmont, Taranaki, lithograph after John Gully, 1875. *Hocken Library*

Page 13. "Forest in the Papakura District", engraving after Dr C. Fischer. *Alexander Turnbull Library*

Page 15. "Site of the Terraces after the Eruption", 1886 oil by Charles Blomfield. *Auckland Institute and Museum*

CHAPTER TWO

Page 19. View of Waikato farmland, watercolour by John Barr Clark Hoyte. *Auckland City Art Gallery*

Pages 20-21. "Tu Kaitote, the pah of Te Wherowhero, on the Waikato", lithograph after G. F. Angas. *Alexander Turnbull Library*

Page 22. "Interior of a Native Village, or 'Pah', in New Zealand", lithograph after J. A. Gilfillan. *National Museum*

Page 23. Maori village in the King Country, oil by W. G. Baker. *National Museum*

Page 25. View of Wanganui, 1857 watercolour by Joseph Hamley. *British Museum*

Pages 26-27. "Waitohi Harbour and Pa 1847", watercolour by William Fox. *Alexander Turnbull Library*

Page 29. Port Nicholson and Petone, lithograph after Charles Heaphy. *Auckland City Art Gallery*

Pages 30-31. Auckland from Mount Hobson, watercolour by Hope. *Auckland City Art Gallery*

Page 33. "Otira Gorge, West Coast Road", 1877 lithograph after Charles Decimus Barraud. *Alexander Turnbull Library*

Pages 34-35. "View of Nelson Haven in Tasman's Gulf", 1841 watercolour by Charles Heaphy. *Alexander Turnbull Library*

Page 37. "The Southern Alps: View from the Mouth of the Arahura or Brunner River on the West Coast", lithograph after Charles Heaphy. *Alexander Turnbull Library*

Pages 38-39. "Dr Greenwood's House in Motueka", 1852 watercolour by Sarah Greenwood. *Alexander Turnbull Library*

Page 41. "Plain of the Ruamahanga, opening into Palliser Bay near Wellington", 1847 engraving after S. C. Brees. *Alexander Turnbull Library*

Pages 42-43. Eketahuna, 1891 watercolour by C. Aubrey. *Alexander Turnbull Library*

Page 44. "View of Native Settlement from our Front Window", ink-and-watercolour by A. J. Cooper. *Alexander Turnbull Library*

Page 45. "The Taieri Plains 1867", watercolour by George O'Brien. *Hocken Library*

Pages 46-47. "Canterbury Plains from Sumner", oil by Archibald Nicoll. *Auckland City Art Gallery*

Page 49. "The Wharf, Collingwood, about the 'sixties'", copy from original watercolour by unknown artist. *Alexander Turnbull Library*

CHAPTER THREE

Page 52. The first Anglican mission settlement, Rangihoua, watercolour by unknown artist. *National Library of Australia/Nan Kivell Collection.*

Pages 54-55. "The meeting of the artist with the wounded chief Hongi, Bay of Islands, November 1827", oil by Augustus Earle. *Alexander Turnbull Library*

Page 57. View of falls near Kerikeri, 1826 lithograph after Lejeune and Chazall. *Alexander Turnbull Library*

Pages 58-59. "Town of Kororarika Bay of Islands", engraving after S. C. Brees. *Alexander Turnbull Library*

Page 61. "Entrance to the Bay of Islands", 1827-8 watercolour by Augustus Earle. *Alexander Turnbull Library*

Pages 62-63. "View of the Missionary House, Waimate, New Zealand", watercolour by Thomas Gardiner. *Alexander Turnbull Library*

Page 65. The C.M.S. station at Kerikeri, 1826 lithograph after Lejeune and Chazall. *Alexander Turnbull Library*

Page 66. View of the settlement at Otaki, 1852 watercolour by William A. McCleverty. *British Museum*

Page 67. "Kororareka, Bay of Islands", watercolour by Mrs Woods. *Auckland Institute and Museum*

Page 69. "Old Mission House and Farm Moturoa About 1870", watercolour by unknown artist. *Taranaki Museum*

Page 71. "Wahapu, New Zealand", watercolour by John Williams. *Aelxander Turnbull Library*

CHAPTER FOUR

Page 74. "View in Queen Charlottes Sound, New Zealand", 1809 aquatint after John Webber. *Alexander Turnbull Library*

Page 77. The *Astrolabe* in French Pass, lithograph after Louis-Auguste de Sainson, 1827. *Alexander Turnbull Library*

Page 79. Loading spars on the Hokianga, watercolour by Charles Heaphy. *Alexander Turnbull Library*

Pages 80-81. "Kororadika Beach", 1832 lithograph after Augustus Earle. *National Library of Australia/Nan Kivell Collection*

Page 83. "Whalers in Port Otago", 1846 lithograph after L. le Breton. *Hocken Library*

Page 85. "Queen Street Auckland 1843", watercolour by Edward Ashworth. *Auckland Institute and Museum*

Page 86. Gillett's whaling station on Kapiti Island, 1844 watercolour by J. A. Gilfillan. *Alexander Turnbull Library*

Page 87. "Mr Rhodes' Station, Acheron Bay, Canterbury", watercolour by William Fox. *Hocken Library*

Page 89. "Lyttelton N.Z. 10 Jan. 1851 Immigration Barracks", watercolour by William Fox. *Hocken Library*

Page 91. "The Mangles Grass Valley on the Teraumai River", 1846 watercolour by William Fox. *Alexander Turnbull Library*

Page 92. "Hokitika River", 1877 lithograph after Charles Decimus Barraud. *Alexander Turnbull Library*

Page 93. "Committee at Pata Pata, Coromandel Harbour", 1852 watercolour by Charles Heaphy. *British Museum*

Page 95. Lake Manapouri, oil by W. G. Baker. *Taranaki Museum*

CHAPTER FIVE

Page 98. "Te Aro Flat from near Captain Sharpes Residence", 1847 engraving after S. C. Brees. *Alexander Turnbull Library*

Page 98. The Aglionby Arms, Hutt Valley, 1847 engraving after S. C. Brees. *Alexander Turnbull Library*

Page 99. "Kai Warra Warra Saw Mill", 1847 engraving after S. C. Brees. *Alexander Turnbull Library*

Page 100. "Looking East from Ponsonby", 1877 watercolour by Sam Stuart. *Auckland City Art Gallery*

Page 101. View of Nelson, 1845 watercolour by F. D. Bell. *W. F. Airey*

Page 103. View of New Plymouth, 1847-8 watercolour by F. D. Bell. *W. F. Airey*

Page 105. "Motueka Valley near Nelson", engraving after A. Campbell.

Page 107. Paekakariki, 1883 oil by John Gully. *National Art Gallery*

Page 109. View of Mercer, 1875 watercolour by Alfred Sharpe. *Auckland Institute and Museum*

Page 111. "The Spit, Napier", 1860 sepia wash by Charles Decimus Barraud. *Alexander Turnbull Library*

Page 113. "Ahiraranga, Mohaka", 1861 watercolour by A. J. Cooper. *Alexander Turnbull Library*

Page 114. View of New Plymouth, watercolour by Lieutenant-Colonel Charles E. Gold. *Alexander Turnbull Library*

CHAPTER SIX